THE DEE BRESTIN
BIBLE STUDY SERIES

A WOMAN
OF
Purpose

David C Cook®
transforming lives together

The Dee Brestin Series
From David C. Cook

BOOKS

The Friendships of Women
The Friendships of Women Devotional Journal

We Are Sisters
We Are Sisters Devotional Journal

BIBLE STUDY GUIDES

A WOMAN OF LOVE
Using Our Gift for Intimacy (Ruth)

A WOMAN OF FAITH
Overcoming the World's Influences (Esther)

A WOMAN OF CONFIDENCE
Triumphing over Life's Trials (1 Peter)

A WOMAN OF PURPOSE
Walking with Jesus (Luke)

A WOMAN OF WORSHIP
Praying with Power (10 Psalms with a music CD)

A WOMAN OF HOSPITALITY
Loving the Biblical Approach (Topical)

A WOMAN OF MODERATION
Breaking the Chains of Poor Eating Habits (Topical)

A WOMAN OF CONTENTMENT
Insight into Life's Sorrows (Ecclesiastes)

A WOMAN OF BEAUTY
Becoming More Like Jesus (1, 2, 3 John)

A WOMAN OF WISDOM
God's Practical Advice for Living (Proverbs)

A WOMAN OF HEALTHY RELATIONSHIPS
Sisters, Mothers, Daughters, Friends (Topical)

THE FRIENDSHIPS OF WOMEN BIBLE STUDY GUIDE
correlates with THE FRIENDSHIPS OF WOMEN

A WOMAN OF PURPOSE
Published by David C. Cook
4050 Lee Vance View
Colorado Springs, CO 80918 U.S.A.

David C. Cook Distribution Canada
55 Woodslee Avenue, Paris, Ontario, Canada N3L 3E5

David C. Cook U.K., Kingsway Communications
Eastbourne, East Sussex BN23 6NT, England

David C. Cook and the graphic circle C logo
are registered trademarks of Cook Communications Ministries.

ISBN 978-0-7814-4334-0

Interior Design: Nancy L. Haskins
Cover Design: Greg Jackson, Thinkpen Design, llc
Cover Photo: ©2007 iStockphoto

Printed in the United States of America
First Edition 2007

3 4 5 6 7 8 9 10 11 12 13

Contents

Acknowledgments 5

Introduction 6

**Special Instructions
for Preparation and Discussion** 8

THE FIRST OASIS: The Savior's Birth
1. First Stop! Elizabeth: Blameless and Barren   Luke 1 11
2. Second Stop! Mary Believed God   Luke 1 19
3. Third Stop! Detectives for the Divine   Luke 2 27

THE SECOND OASIS: The Savior's Power
4. Fourth Stop! Who Is This Who Even Forgives Sins?   Luke 7 38
5. Fifth Stop! Who Is This Who Stops Storms?   Luke 8—9 47

THE THIRD OASIS: The Savior's Wisdom
6. Sixth Stop! Mary of Bethany   Luke 10 58
7. Seventh Stop! Praying Effectively   Luke 11 69
8. Eighth Stop! Fear God and Nothing Else   Luke 12 82
9. Ninth Stop! Parables That Women Love   Luke 15 90

THE FOURTH OASIS: The Savior's Victory
10. Tenth Stop! The Savior's Farewell   Luke 22 100
11. Eleventh Stop! Do Not Weep for Me   Luke 23 109
12. Last Stop! A Slow Dawning   Luke 24 118

Sources 125

Leader's Helps available at
http://www.davidccook.com/catalog/Detail.cfm?sn=104583&source=search

To my sister Sally,

who led me to the Savior.

How I Thank God For:

Dr. Darrell L. Bock of Dallas Seminary
Whose award-winning commentaries on Luke are the best I have ever used and have profoundly impacted this guide. Whose support and counsel in reading and commenting upon this manuscript has been of inestimable value to me and to the women doing this study.

The team at NexGen in Colorado Springs
Who listen to the Lord, to each other, and to me

My team at home in Nebraska
Particularly Gay Tillotson for dozens of vital tasks done well and enthusiastically.

The reflective and diligent women in my Sonrise Bible Study
for testing this study and then vulnerably allowing me to read their answers.

My precious family

Introduction

Did you know that Luke is the Gospel that is most empathetic to women?

Luke alone gives us detail into the birth of Christ from Mary's perspective. We learn how God astonished her through Gabriel's visit, provided her with a mentor in Elizabeth, and amazed her with miracles that she kept "pondering in her heart." In Luke alone we read of Jesus raising a widow's only son; of a sinful woman who broke her alabaster bottle at his feet; and of the women who traveled with Him and supported Him out of their means. In Luke alone we read of Martha rebuking her sister Mary and of Jesus defending Mary. And (my favorite) we read of the women being first at the tomb, running out to tell the men, and the men saying that the women's words seemed like nonsense! (The word that Luke the physician actually used to describe the women's talk means "the delirious talk of the very ill!")

Why is Luke's Gospel filled with many incidents concerning women that don't occur in Matthew, Mark, and John? Luke tells us he received his historical account from eyewitnesses. Who were those eyewitnesses? The apostles—definitely. But historians consider the possibility that Luke received much of his information from Mary, the mother of Jesus, and from the devout company of women who traveled with the Twelve and helped to support them out of their means (Luke 8:1–3). Why do I, as a woman, identify with so many passages in Luke? Perhaps it is because women may have been a primary source. Perhaps it is because Luke shows so clearly how Jesus valued women, reached out to women, used women for vital messages, and understood women's deepest longings. We are not less valuable than men, as Jesus makes abundantly clear (particularly in Luke!) He has a purpose for our lives. Just as He allowed women to be a vital part of His ministry when He walked on earth, He calls you and me to be an active part of His ministry now.

Susannah Wesley exhorted women not to live their lives as the rest of humankind, who pass through the world like straws upon a river, which are carried which way the stream or wind drives them. How can we be transformed into women of purpose? It begins by beholding the Savior. Just as the women who spent time beholding Jesus in Luke's Gospel were transformed into women of purpose, so will you be.

Beholding takes slowing down. I remember that in high school I didn't particular enjoy history. I memorized lots of dates, places, and people for the exams, and then promptly forgot them. Boring. But then, in college, history was studied in a whole different way. Instead of this vast overview, we really looked into the life of Thomas Jefferson, reading biographies. Suddenly, he began to seem like a real person to me instead of just a name, a date, and a place. I was fascinated. If that is true of Thomas Jefferson, how much more should we slow down and behold the Savior.

I also remember a whirlwind trip I took with my dear dad through England, Scotland, and Wales. The week is a blur in my memory except for one day when I persuaded Dad to slow down and spend the whole day exploring Oxford and the places significant to C. S. Lewis. We walked along the hill Lewis was on when he was converted, we sat in halls in which he taught, we lunched in a pub in which he debated theology, and we closed our day by standing at the head-stone where his body was buried. That day is a golden memory, worth the price of the whole trip, and because of it, both C. S. Lewis and my dad are even more precious to me than before!

I don't want the Savior, or Luke's Gospel (or the women in your small group!) to be a blur in your memory. Though you will read two chapters of Luke each week so that you will "drive" through all of Luke, we will "get out of the car" and walk slowly through four oasis stops.

We also can only see as the Spirit takes the veil from our eyes. How I encourage you to ask God each day: "Father, please help me to see what You have for me today!"

Luke describes more unique incidents involving women than any other Gospel writer. Here is in an incident from Luke 7 where Jesus is moved with compassion for a widow whose only son has died. Jesus raised him from the dead, giving him back to his mother.

Special Instructions for Preparation and Discussion

Once, while being interviewed, the Omaha radio announcer tried to provoke me by saying: "I doubt very much that any serious growth occurs in women's Bible studies—they are simply glorified times for women to gab over coffee." I was able to share with him (most graciously, of course) that, in my present study, the women had memorized John 15, had done their homework, and were sharing vulnerably, as many men are hesitant to do, from their hearts. Either gender can use Bible study time poorly, but there are certain standards you can set right now to prevent that:

1. Do your homework—each day, same time, same place, for a minimum of 30 minutes! Each day, ask God to speak to you through His Word. If you don't have a hymnal, buy one. Every home needs a Bible and a hymnal. Certain hymns for your times with God will be suggested.

2. In the discussion, be sensitive to the Spirit. The naturally talkative need to exercise control and the shy need to exercise courage and speak up.

3. Stay on target in the discussions. These lessons can be discussed in 90 minutes. If you don't have that much time, you have two options:
    A. Divide the lessons. Do the prayer exercise both weeks.
    B. Do the whole lesson but discuss half the questions.

4. Follow the instructions for group prayer at the close of each lesson. Keep confidences in the group. There is power when we pray together.

May you rejoice, as Mary did, in the realization that God is mindful of you (Luke 1:46–48).

The Savior's Birth

*So they hurried off and found Mary
and Joseph, and the baby, who was
lying in the manger.*
—Luke 2:16

The Savior's Birth

(Luke 1—2)

The church of my childhood was not Bible-centered, though exceptions were made at Christmas and Easter. At Christmas, we always read the second chapter of Luke and sang carols based on this hauntingly beautiful passage. (Luke alone tells the intimate details of Jesus' birth.) Therefore, when I was confronted with the claims of Christ as a young wife and mother, I had to decide whether Jesus was a fairy tale or God incarnate. I prayed and cried out to God to show me the truth. The images which kept flooding my mind and which caused me to pursue the truth were the majestic scenes from the birth: the glory of the Lord shining around the terrified shepherds; the announcement of the sign: a baby wrapped in swaddling clothes and lying in a manger; and the angelic message: "Do not be afraid. I bring you good news of great joy! . . . Today in the town of David a Savior has been born to you; He is Christ the Lord."

Since Luke's birth account was pivotal in bringing me to Christ, it is dear to me. But the longer I looked at this tapestry, the more I saw that touched me as a woman. The story begins tenderly with the births of two babies: first, John the Baptist, then, the Christ Child. And woven into this tapestry is also the account of the God-ordained friendship of their two mothers. Come with me to spend a few weeks at the oasis of "The Savior's Birth."

First Stop!

Elizabeth: Blameless and Barren

Who of us does not long for special friends to love and to be loved by? God knows our longings as women—for He is the One who created us to be the relational sex! He also brings friends across our path who can particularly minister to our unique needs and to whom we can minister. But we need to be alert, as Elizabeth was to Mary, and as Mary was to Elizabeth.

I would encourage you to be alert to the women in this small group—for God may have placed someone here especially with you in mind. Ask God to give you discernment. Author and speaker Win Couchman says: "Sometimes when I first meet an interesting woman I have a lust to acquire her as a friend—like a possession. But if I pray—God may completely change my attitude, and my motive becomes purer, or, I find myself drawn to a different woman!" So pray. Plead for discernment! God knows your needs better than you do.

In addition, notice that God is more likely to anoint those whose hearts are blameless toward Him and who are stepping out in faith. See how this is true in Elizabeth's life. God used her mightily as a mentor to Mary.

Prepare Your Heart to Hear

Before each of the following five devotional times, quiet your heart and ask God to speak to you personally from His Word.

Memory Work

In this birth oasis you will memorize Luke 1:46–50. This week begin with verses 46 and 47:

And Mary said: "My soul praises the Lord and my spirit rejoices in God my Savior."

WARMUP

Share your name and why you came to this group. Was Jesus a part of your childhood Advents or Christmases? If so, what memory stands out?

DAY 1
. . . .

Overview

Read Luke 1—2.

1. Read all of the introductory notes. Comment on what stood out to you from:
   A. The Introduction (p. 7)

   B. The Special Instructions for Preparation and Discussion (p. 8)

   C. The introduction for THE FIRST OASIS: The Savior's Birth (p. 10)

   D. The introduction for The First Stop! Elizabeth: Blameless and Barren (p. 11)

Spend five minutes on the memory passage.

Often doing a word at a time will help to cement it in your mind:
- Luke
- Luke 1
- Luke 1:46–50
- Luke 1:46–50 "And …
- Luke 1:46–50 "And Mary …etc.

DAY 2
. . . .

Introducing Elizabeth: Barren, yet Blameless

God's Word is clear that part of His purpose for us is to mentor the younger women in our lives (Titus 2:3–5). Older women are called, but we are all older than someone. How transformed your life will be if you, like Elizabeth, are open to the younger women who come across your path.

Likewise, we should each be seeking out mentors. How much more fruitful your life will be if you choose your friends wisely. Mary was very wise to make the long journey to Elizabeth's home. One of the ways you can tell if a woman is truly godly is to see how she has responded to difficulty in her life. Elizabeth, as you will see, was barren, yet blameless. She trusted God when He didn't make sense, and God called her to mentor a woman for whom there would be many times when He would not make sense.

2. Read Luke 1 again, looking for evidences that implied Elizabeth knew and trusted God. Record the verse and why you believe it shows an intimacy with God.

Elizabeth was blameless in God's sight. This does not mean that she was perfect but, as *The Message* paraphrases it, that she "enjoyed a clear conscience before God." This begins by coming to God in salvation, by putting our trust in the payment that God provided through Jesus on the cross. Isaiah 1:18 gives us the following word picture of what happens to a person in God's sight when he puts his trust in Christ:

> *Though your sins are like scarlet,*
> *they shall be as white as snow.*

3. What do you learn about living a holy and blameless life from the following passages?

A. 1 John 1:7–9 *Living in light of ~~chosen~~ cleansed in blood of Jesus. I am a sinner.*

B. Philippians 2:14–16 *Stay away from complaining & arguing. Hold tightly to the word of life.*

C. 1 Thessalonians 5:23 *may God make me holy in every way and may my spirit, soul & body be blameless till Lord Jesus comes again.*

Our son John and daughter-in-law Julie struggled with bringing a baby to term. I never knew how much barrenness hurt until it happened to our family. One of the things I feared was that John and Julie would stop trusting God. They were trying to live whole-heartedly for Him—so why was this happening?

One day John said to me: "Mom, if God never gives us a baby, we will trust Him."

"Why?"

"Because He died for us."

How we need to remember this truth in dark times. Elizabeth probably came to the point in her life when she assumed she would never be a mother.

Was it because of sin in her life?

Was it because God did not love her?

Was it because God was not able to give her children?

No! No! No! Elizabeth was barren because God had a plan she could not see. He has a purpose for her life far beyond her imaginings.

Like John and Julie, Elizabeth looked at the character of God and chose to trust Him in the dark.

4. In Luke 1, what two words beginning with "b" are used to describe Elizabeth? What does the juxtaposition of these two words teach you?

barren & blessed

5. A. Have you ever been or are you being denied a deep desire of your heart? Have you faced times when God did not make sense? What were your feelings?

I run to him in my confusion for his comfort & grace.

   B. What can you learn from saints of the past, like Job, Elizabeth, and others who trusted God in the dark?

Keep on keep on - don't give up.

6. What do the following verses tell you about the character of God which could help you when He is not making sense?

   A. 1 Peter 5:7 *This life is not all there is. Eternal life will come and it will be more then anything we can imagine.*

   B. Ecclesiastes 3:11 *We must trust him now & do his work on earth. We cannot see the plan from beginning to end.*

Review your memory passage.

Horatio Spafford wrote the words to "It Is Well with My Soul" after surveying the place in the ocean where his four daughters drowned. Sing this hymn from your hymnal in your private devotional time

DAY 2

The Greeting Scene

God often seems to zoom His camera in on greeting scenes and parting scenes—significant moments in relationships. This greeting scene has been painted by artists through the centuries, captured in poetry, and reflected on by believers often, especially, at Christmas.

7. Why might Mary's appearance have surprised Elizabeth?

Because it was coming to pass as the Holy Spirit had told her.

8. What two things, according to Luke 1:41, happened to Elizabeth? How might this have made her feel? *Child leaped inside of her & she was filled with the holy spirit. High as a kite.*

9. Describe all the truths that you can find that the Holy Spirit revealed to Elizabeth in verses 42–45. *Mother of the Lord visiting her. Mary blessed because she believed.*

10. Why did John the Baptist leap in Elizabeth's womb, according to the prophecy given to Elizabeth? What do you think this means?

Joy of the coming of the Lord Jesus

We will be studying many narrative passages in Luke, for Gospels are made up, primarily, of narratives. One important principle in interpreting a narrative passage is that our interpretation and application should not contradict a didactic (teaching) passage, for the Bible is its own best interpreter. For example, we could not conclude that when we are filled with the Holy Spirit we will be able to prophesy (as Elizabeth did) or that we will be with child (as Mary was)—for teaching passages do not support this, but rather, teach otherwise. This is how false teaching can occur, by inferring something from a narrative passage that is not supported by teaching passages.

However, sometimes we can infer things, even though it may not be the central point of the passage, as long as those inferences are not contradicted but rather supported by teaching passages. For example, though the central point of the greeting scene between Mary and Elizabeth is to show us how carefully God had planned the Savior's birth—even preparing His mother through Elizabeth's prophecy, even preparing John the Baptist—we can also infer, from this greeting scene, some things about blessing others that is indeed, supported by didactic teaching elsewhere in Scripture.

11. How does Elizabeth bless Mary in each of the following verses? What might you learn from Elizabeth about blessing others?

A. Luke 1:42

Glad cry

B. Luke 1:43

Honor-humility that Mary would visit her.

C. Luke 1:44

Baby jumped for joy.

D. Luke 1:45

Blessed

12. How might you apply what you've seen about blessing others to someone in your life today? Be specific. *Glad cry, cards, sharing in joy, true to heart happiness to that person.*

DAY 3

A Godly Wife

Some couples are in a negative cycle. One criticizes, the other responds in kind, and round it goes! Hearts harden in this kind of marriage. When Zechariah doubted God, we see no evidence of disrespect on Elizabeth's part. She seems to overlook his weakness in love. She believes in him and supports him.

Read Luke 1:6–25 again.

13. What strengths and weaknesses do you see in Elizabeth's husband, Zechariah?

Obeidance   doubt
loved God
kind

14. How did God discipline Zechariah for the doubting words he spoke to Gabriel? What thoughts and feelings do you think Zechariah had as he was deaf and dumb for the following nine months?

Read Luke 1:57–80.

15. Find clues in Luke 1:57–80 for:

   A. Elizabeth and Zechariah's positive relationship

   B. Zechariah's teachable heart

16. What can a woman do to draw her husband closer to God? What mistakes do wives make that may harden their husbands' hearts?

17. If you are married, what are some of the strengths you see in your husband? What godly characteristics?

   A. List them—and tell him about them today!

   B. What are some ways you could help a close married friend to think well of her husband?

Read Matthew 1:18–25.

18. A. How did Joseph react similarly to Zechariah?

   B. How did God help Joseph to believe?

19. Imagine that Mary confided in Elizabeth that Joseph was having trouble believing God. What reassuring words, based on her experience and faith, might Elizabeth have given to Mary?

DAY 4
. . . .

Elizabeth's Heart

How do you feel when someone is greatly blessed by God? Often that is a true test of our character! Elizabeth is pregnant with John the Baptist, but here comes this teenager who is pregnant with the Messiah! Yet there is not an inkling of jealousy, but only pure joy and excitement. Elizabeth seems truly focused on God's praise, so she can rejoice with Mary.

Meditate on Luke 1:39–45 again.

20. A. What qualities do you see in Elizabeth through this greeting scene?

B. Why, in your opinion, wasn't Elizabeth jealous?

21. Elizabeth's humility, her desire to elevate Jesus, can be seen in Elizabeth's son as well.

    A. Give evidence for that based on Luke 3:15–17.

    B. What evidence can others see in your life for your desire to elevate Jesus?

Personal Action Assignment

Today, follow the example of Elizabeth. Keep a clear conscience by responding quickly to the Holy Spirit. Just as we cannot save ourselves, we cannot live the Christian life in our own strength. When the Spirit calls, respond! Either in the space provided or in your journal, record times you respond or times when you disobeyed. Try to do it right after it occurs. We'll ask for reflections on this exercise next week. For example, this is my journal for yesterday.

6 a.m. Wanted to stay in bed but I did remember to respond to the Spirit. Got up and went right to work-out at the Y—listened to sermon by R. C. Sproul on my iPod.

8:30 a.m. Time in prayer. Asked Him for guidance for the day—sensed I should write and encourage an elderly widowed friend. Did it right away.

2:30 p.m. Worrying about money, tried to turn it over to the Lord. Help me, Lord.

4 p.m. Listened to gossip and was silent. Should have said something positive about that friend—or done something besides be silent. Forgive me, Lord.

7 p.m. Obeyed His prompting to shut off television and read. Am getting into a good Francine Rivers novel. Thank You!

9 p.m. His Spirit told me not to grab that handful of chips before bed but I did anyhow. Forgive me, Lord. Help me not be deceived.

YOUR TURN:

Review your memory verse.

DAY 5
....

God Cared for Elizabeth

Jesus promises that if we put Him first, He will meet our needs (Luke 12:31). Every single one of us has the need to be loved, to belong, and to feel that our life has a purpose.
Review Luke 1:5–8; 1:23–25; and 1:39–58.

22. As you review the above narrative passages, what evidence can you find that Elizabeth put God first, that she sought Him, and that she trusted Him?

Elizabeth's five-month seclusion probably had a spiritual motive, as evidenced by Luke 1:25.

23. As you review the above passages, what evidence do you find for God's love for Elizabeth?

24. What evidence do you find for the love of her family and friends?

25. What evidence can you find that God had a purpose for Elizabeth?

26. One purpose for every older woman (and we are all older than someone) is specified in Titus 2:3–5. List the things we are called to be and to teach.

27. In what ways do you see Elizabeth fulfilling the above?

28. What are some of the greatest needs in your life right now? What could you learn from this lesson that is helpful in regard to your needs?

29. If time permits, share one thing God has impressed on you from this lesson. (Give women the freedom to pass.)

Prayer Time

Many people are intimidated by the idea of praying out loud. This guide will gently lead you into this gradually. And no one will ever be forced to pray out loud.

Elizabeth encouraged Mary by affirming her faith, by blessing her. Today, stand in a circle holding hands. Each woman will bless the woman on her right in prayer. She might say something like: "Thank You for Cindy—for her gentleness." If she doesn't know Cindy, she can say, "Lord, bless Cindy." If she doesn't want to speak out loud, she can bless Cindy silently and squeeze Cindy's hand. Then Cindy will bless the woman on her right.

Second Stop!

Mary Believed God

How many sermons have you heard about Mary? Evangelicals and Protestants tend to neglect her, TO OUR GREAT LOSS! She, alone among women, was chosen to be the mother of the Messiah.

Gabriel tells Mary she has found favor (*charis*) or grace, with God. Dr. Darrell L. Bock explains that "favor signifies God's gracious choice of someone through whom God does something special (Noah is spared from the Flood; Gideon is chosen to judge Israel; Hannah is given a child in barrenness …)."[1]

Can we do something to receive favor from God? Scripture is clear that our righteousness is pitiful when compared to a Holy God (Isa. 64:6). If there is anything good in us, it comes through trusting God. As you look at Noah, Abraham, Hannah, and Mary, you will find one common quality—they believed God. In Luke's Gospel you will repeatedly see that it is faith that pleases Jesus. For example, Jesus commends the bleeding woman who touched His cloak, saying, "Daughter, your faith has healed you. Go in peace" (Luke 8:48). Likewise, Mary demonstrates faith when her immediate response, in sharp contrast to Zechariah's, is faith. And Elizabeth, when prophesying through the power of the Spirit, says to Mary: "Blessed is she who has believed that what the Lord has said to her will be accomplished!" (Luke 1:45)

R. C. Sproul says there is a great difference between believing in God and believing God. Mary, as we will see, did both. What would happen in your life if you believed God as Mary did and acted on your mustard seed of faith?

Prepare Your Heart to Hear

Before each of the following five devotional times, quiet your heart and ask God to speak to you personally from His Word. Then, like Mary, trust that He will!

Memory Work

Add Luke 1:48 to Luke 1:46–47.

> *And Mary said: "My soul glorifies the Lord and my spirit rejoices in God my Savior, for he has been mindful of the humble state of his servant. From now on all generations will call me blessed."*

WARMUP

Mary and Elizabeth's story is a wonderful example of how being aware of the leading of the Spirit can help you discover an amazing friendship. Can you think of a time when someone came into your life, and you now believe it may have been a "divine encounter"? Looking back, what makes you think God may have led you together?

DAY 1
· ·

Overview

Read Luke 3-4.

1. Read over the introductory notes for The Second Stop! Mary Believed God (p. 19). What stood out to you?

As an overview, read Luke 1:26–56.

Spend five minutes on the memory passage.

DAY 2
· ·

Mary Exercised Her Faith

In some liturgical churches, the "Annunciation" is celebrated on the 25th of March. "Annunciation" means "to announce, to bring tidings." Gabriel announced to Mary that she would be "overshadowed by the Holy Spirit" to conceive Jesus. John 1 makes it clear this was not the beginning of Jesus' life, but simply the beginning of His time in the flesh. The Word made flesh, a paradox poets have pondered. John Donne calls it "immensity cloistered in a womb." Luci Shaw describes the enigma as "the Word, stern sentenced to be nine months dumb."[2]

Read Luke 1:26–38.

2. Try to get to know Mary through the following verses. List anything you discover or *discern* about her.

A. Luke 1:26–28

B. Luke 1:29

C. Luke 1:30–33

D. Luke 1:34

E. Luke 1:35–37

F. Luke 1:38

G. Luke 1:39

3. Sometimes, though we believe in God, we have trouble trusting and obeying. We will skip ahead for a moment to a section in Luke 17 where the disciples had trouble trusting.

A. Read Luke 17:1–4. Jesus warns against offending the faith of others, and then, in verses 3 and 4, gives a command that overwhelms the disciples with its difficulty. What is it?

B. Why can this command be so difficult to obey?

C. How do the disciples respond to this difficult saying in Luke 17:5?

D. Why does it take *faith* to truly forgive someone who has hurt you?

E. What does Jesus tell them in Luke 17:6? How is this an answer to Luke 17:5?

It is not that we need more faith, but we must exercise what faith we have.

F. Is there an area of your life where you have trouble trusting God? How could you *exercise* "the mustard seed" of faith that you already have?

Mary provides us with a beautiful example of exercising her faith. There were certain things she knew to be true of God, and she acted on them. Each time she did that, God met her, which, in turn, helped her to trust Him more.

4. Look at Luke 1:29–34 again:

A. What did Gabriel tell Mary that could have been hard to believe?

B. What was Mary's response in verse 34?

C. What contrast do you see between Zechariah's response to Gabriel's and Mary's response to Gabriel? (vv. 18, 34)

Zechariah doubted that it could happen. Mary simply wanted to know *how* it would happen. Luci Shaw says that Mary was asking God to "widen her imagination." Mary knew God could do it, she just couldn't imagine *how*, since she was a virgin. So she asked Him to "widen her imagination." I have done that when I am facing a fear. For example, though it may sound silly, I worry about my husband Steve, who died last October. I know Steve is with the Lord, but I worry that he is sad, because I'm sad. I worry that he misses us, for we surely miss him. Yet I also know that God promises that in heaven He will wipe away every tear from our eyes. So, I ask God to "widen my imagination." *How* can Steve be happy when we are sad and parted from him? I know I can't know for certain, but I think the Spirit is telling me that now Steve knows so much more than I do, so he has a comfort, peace, and even an excitement for us.

D. What "sign" does Gabriel give Mary in Luke 1:36 to help her believe?

E. How does Mary then "exercise" the small mustard seed of faith she has? (vv. 38–39)

F. Look at a Bible map and estimate how far Mary walked in order to visit Elizabeth. (Mary lived in Nazareth and Elizabeth in the hill country outside of Jerusalem.) To put yourself in Mary's shoes, name a destination from your home of similar distance. (If there is a route that goes through hilly country, choose it!)

G. Those who walked covered about 20 miles a day. How long did this take Mary?

H. Considering the length and difficulty of this trip, why do you think Mary went?

5. Reviewing what you learned about Elizabeth last week, list some of the reasons why God may have wanted Mary to spend time with her.

6. When facing a difficult situation, do you consider a godly older woman who has been where you are going and done it well? Or do you automatically run to a peer?

7. Share a time when you believed God and acted on it and were blessed. Perhaps it was in friendship, or mothering, or another area. Be specific.

DAY 3

The Greeting Scene

In *The Book of God: The Bible as a Novel,* Walter Wangerin, Jr. imagines the following thoughts and feelings in Mary and Elizabeth during their amazing greeting scene:

> *Zechariah didn't hear the knock. Zechariah wouldn't have heard a hammer on his anvil or thunder in the heavens. Ever since the night of his "vision of angels," as he described it in writing for her—the old nailsmith had been completely deaf and dumb.*
>
> *So Elizabeth opened her door herself—and there stood her nephew's child, Joachim's little girl, whom she had not seen in years. "Mary!" Elizabeth cried. "Pretty Mary, it's you! But you're alone!"*
>
> *But this was no common visit.*
>
> *And Mary was not a child anymore.*
>
> *Her dark brows were lifted in an intense appeal, and her eyes were filled with beseeching. Clearly, she had come with a question.*
>
> *Then several things happened so swiftly that they were all one thing, and that thing was the revelation of God.*
>
> *Mary's eyes dropped to Elizabeth's breasts and then to her belly. In the softest of whispers, she said, "Hail, Elizabeth."*
>
> *Immediately the baby in Elizabeth's womb leaped up to her heart, and old Elizabeth shrieked.*
>
> *Because Elizabeth suddenly understood everything: the child inside of her, the reason for Mary's appearing, the glory of the days in which they were living, the great thing that God was starting to do!*
>
> *"Oh, Mary!" Elizabeth cried. She grabbed her young niece by both her arms and pulled her into the house. "Mary, blessed are you among women, and blessed is the fruit of your womb!"*
>
> *Mary mouthed the words, My womb?* [3]

8. What impresses you about Wangerin's description. ? Do you agree or not?

9. Go through Elizabeth's greeting again and imagine how each of the following verses impacted and blessed Mary.

   A. Luke 1:42

   B. Luke 1:43

   C. Luke 1:44

   D. Luke 1:45

10. How can you see through the above that God cared for Mary's needs in sending her to Elizabeth? What does this mean, personally, to you?

DAY 4
• •

The Magnificat

When a significant event happens in biblical history, God provides a song. Mary's response, her "Magnificat," has been used in public liturgies over the centuries. Contemporary praise choruses also draw upon Mary's ponderings. Mark Lowry wrote: "Mary, did you know that the One you delivered will soon deliver you?" I believe her Magnificat shows that, yes, she at least understood dimly. Her soul rejoices in God her *Savior*. She seems to know many things, evidencing that she was very familiar with the Psalms, with Hannah's song, and Scripture in general. Her Magnificat is also a beautiful demonstration of the anointing of the Spirit on this woman who found favor with God.

Read Luke 1:46–55.

11. Meditate on the Magnificat.
   A. Luke 1:46–49 Mary praises God for being personal. What are some of the thoughts which overwhelm her?

   B. Mary's words echo the psalmist's words. How do you see this in Psalm 8:3–5? In Psalm 138:6?

   C. How is Mary's song similar to Hannah's song? (See 1 Samuel 2.)

   D. Based on her Magnificat, do you think Mary expected a suffering Savior? Explain.

12. What impresses you most from the Magnificat?

Personal Action Assignment

Write your own song of praise. (Include ways God has been mindful of you, ways you have seen His power and mercy in your life, or in the lives of those from past generations

Close by reflectively singing "Joy to the World," which is actually a song about the second coming of Christ.

DAY 5
. . . .

Mary Stayed Three Months

We are left to imagine what happened during those three months, for Luke does not supply us with those details. Some of the things that I imagine, as a woman, include valuable mentoring time with Elizabeth where Mary watched her and learned how to be a godly wife. I believe they talked about how to raise boys, made blue layettes together, and helped each other find strength in God through prayer, through praise, and through sharing what they knew about prophecy.

Recently I was visiting with a woman who said: "My friends are believers—but all they talk about is their kids and their activities. They don't talk about the Lord or their need for support in overcoming their sinful tendencies. I long for a deeper kind of friendship." Surely Mary and Elizabeth had this in each other. Jesus says that our words reflect the overflow of our hearts. Because Elizabeth and Mary spent so much time alone with the Lord, their words became a fountain of strength to one another. Perhaps Elizabeth shared with Mary some of the things God taught her during her long time of barrenness. There were going to be many times in Mary's future when life would be hard. I imagine that Elizabeth's words came back to help her to face the difficulties of life with trust that God was good and would do all things well in His time.

I also believe that Mary was there when John the Baptist was born even though Luke does not say she was there. (But there are many things we are not told!) We know Elizabeth was a little more than six months pregnant when Mary arrived—and we know Mary stayed three months. It makes sense to me that Mary stayed three months in order to help Elizabeth with the birth and the new baby. I think that is precisely why Mary stayed so long! Mary didn't know that in six months she would be giving birth on a bare barn floor without mother or midwife. But God knew. God knew Mary's needs better than she did. I believe He provided her with the valuable mentoring experience of seeing a baby being born, of seeing the umbilical cord tied and cut, of seeing that baby washed and wrapped in swaddling clothes—because He loved Mary, and He wanted to prepare her.

> *The assertion of Luke that Mary returned home (verse 56) does not necessarily imply that she did not wait for John's birth and circumcision. The probabilities are in favour of supposing that she did so wait, and received the additional consolations which the song of Zacharias was so able to bring back.*[4]
>
> R.M. Edgar in *The Pulpit Commentary*

13. What do you imagine happened during the three months Mary spent with Elizabeth? Why?

14. A. If Mary talked to Joseph before she left, she probably knew that he did not believe her story. How might have Elizabeth provided comfort and strength through her experience?

    B. If you are married, have there been godly older women in your life who have helped you to be a better wife or to give your husband some grace? If so, what did they say or do?

15. Do you have friends who encourage you spiritually when you are with them, as Mary and Elizabeth encouraged each other? If so, what is it about their conversations that strengthens you?

16. Do you think you are an encouragement spiritually to others through your conversation? If so, how? If not, what changes could you make so you are an encouragement?

Prayer Time

One of the best ways to encourage one another spiritually is through prayer. In order to pray effectively for one another, it is important to be honest and vulnerable with one another. Have each woman write down a need in her life on an index card. She can sign the card or leave it unsigned. Then place the cards face down in the center. Each woman should draw a card out and commit to praying for that need all week. (The group needs to commit now to keeping confidences within the group.) In the prayer time next week, give the women an opportunity to share if the needs they wrote on their cards were met.

Third Stop!

Detectives for the Divine

Mary was a ponderer. Repeatedly we are told, "She pondered, or she treasured these things in her heart." *Often the difference between someone who lives a wasted life and someone who lives a fruitful life is that they choose to reflect on the things of God* (Luke 10:42; Ps. 1). In this hurried life, reflective souls are rare—yet we are commanded to "live quiet lives" (1 Tim. 2:2). Is that possible in a day of cell phones, cable television, and church meeting mania?

Yes. Some succeed in choosing the reflective life. They say no to outside voices and carve out reflective times. They do their Bible study thoughtfully, making notes, asking God to speak to them. They know how to ask questions when they read the Bible, to observe, so that they are not just reading, but reflecting, meditating. They keep journals, they read, and they are constantly looking at life as detectives for the Divine.

Will the next generation have individuals who are ponderers? Yes, God has always had a remnant, people like Mary, Simeon, and Anna who seek Him. Many have been trained to seek Him, having had mothers who guarded them from too much television and too many outside activities. These mothers knew that reflective souls need time to read, and to be read to. They need time to converse, to be outdoors in God's creation, and to be still and know that He is God.

Prepare Your Heart to Hear

Before each of the following five devotional times, quiet your heart and ask God to speak to you personally from His Word.

Memory Work

Complete Luke 1:46–50.

> *And Mary said: "My soul glorifies the Lord and my spirit rejoices in God my Savior, for he has been mindful of the humble state of his servant. From now on all generations will call me blessed, for the Mighty One has done great things for me—holy is his name. His mercy extends to those who fear him, from generation to generation."*

WARMUP

Ponder why some women are wonderful detectives for the Divine and others, though believers, miss His voice, His wonder, His deep revelations, and His paths on a daily basis. List everything that might make the difference.

DAY 1

Overview

Read Luke 5—6.

1. Read over the introductory notes for The Third Stop! Detectives for the Divine (p. 27) along with the Scriptures. What stood out to you?

2. Do you think you (and your family) live quiet, reflective lives? If so, what do you do? If not, what might you do differently?

Personal Action Assignment

If you are married, share with your husband what you have been learning about the importance of quiet, reflective times and consider how you are doing as a family. Is the Lord leading you to make any changes? If so, what?

Meditate on Luke 2:19, 51.

Learn the memory passage.

DAY 2

Reflecting on Scripture

Reading Scripture and reflecting on Scripture are very different. Today you are going to be looking at one of the most familiar passages in the whole Bible. Yet, as you practice the art of reflection, you may see things that you didn't see before. Reflective people ask "detective" questions. In narrative passages, which make up a good part of the Gospels, you ask the questions: where, when, who, how, and why. Reflective people put themselves in the place of the people they are reading about and try to imagine how they were feeling and thinking. This means reading between the lines, using cross-references, observing, observing, and observing. This will make the passage come alive.

3. Read Luke 2:1–7. Be a detective for the divine by asking where, when, why, how, and what. The Bible is its own best commentary, so use cross-references, a concordance, and Bible maps. Continually put yourself in Mary's place to imagine what she was feeling and thinking. Often your questions will simply lead to more questions—but that's wonderful. Questions help you think, and thinking helps you see.

A. WHERE: (Questions you might ask yourself: How far would they travel from Nazareth to Bethlehem? Where else is Bethlehem mentioned in Scripture—Who else lived there? Use a concordance. What was Bethlehem like?) Find out everything you can about WHERE.

B. WHEN: (Questions you might ask yourself: What phrases in this passage have to do with time? Why do you think Jesus was born at the time of the census?) Find out everything you can about WHEN.

C. WHO: (Questions you might ask yourself: Who is mentioned in this passage? What do you know about them? What phrases are used to describe them in this passage?) The more you discover about WHO the more you will see.

D. HOW: (Questions you might ask yourself: How did God get the Messiah to His prophesied birthplace? How do you think Mary felt about this trip? How do you think she felt when she looked over Bethlehem? How did she bring forth her first-born son with no mother or midwife?) Let your imagination go with HOW.

E. WHY: (Questions you might ask yourself: Why this little town? Why no room in the inn? Why did it come to pass in these days?) Again, let your imagination make you a detective with WHY.

4. Did your observations give you any new insights? If so, what?

Read Luke 2:8–20. Use a paraphrase or fresh translation.

5. Ask questions, use cross-references. See if you can notice something about this familiar passage you haven't seen before.

6. Imagine you were a shepherd. What might your life be like?

The shepherds themselves may have been detectives for the divine. Often those who work outdoors (like shepherds and farmers) are more aware of God. It is difficult (though not impossible) to consider the heavens and not think of God, or to observe the change of seasons, or the instinct of the ant, and *not* think of the Creator. In today's world, particularly in America, we have lost the wonder of the outdoors, riding instead of walking, watching TV instead of nature, and hurrying instead of smelling the roses.

7. Describe the last time nature delighted you. What were you doing? Are you (and your children) outdoors enough or do you need to make changes?

8. Imagine you experienced what the shepherds experienced that night. How might you feel? What might you tell others?

9. Reflective people are also aware of God's sovereignty, that He brings events and people into our lives for a reason. When the shepherds visited Mary, "[she] treasured up all of these things and pondered them in her heart" (Luke 2:19). Pretend you are Mary, journaling, recording evidences for the reality of God in your life. What are some possible entries you might make in your journal after this night?

10. Step back into your own shoes. What evidence for the reality of God in your life might you record from the last few months?

11. Why is it wise to record these things, to keep them in your "treasure chest"? If you are not in the habit of doing this, what small step might you make toward beginning?

> *I keep a journal in which I record times I have spied God in my life. One of the times God was particularly near to me was when my husband was planning to leave me—and when he did. Again and again God reached out through the love of friends, through the ways He was so obviously trying to get my husband's attention, and through His presence, so unmistakingly real, so strong … Now, when the road is lonely and I question, "Was God really with me? Or was it my imagination?" I look back and see, in black and white, that, yes, He was with me.*
>
> Peg, as told in *The Friendships of Women* [5]

DAY 3
Simeon and Anna

Now we come upon two individuals who waited in expectancy for the Messiah. Luke alone tells the story of Simeon and Anna, and of how each of these devout prophets "recognized" this baby as the Messiah. (My two youngest grandchildren are named Simeon and Ana—how I pray they will be like their godly namesakes.) It is so beautiful that God had two representatives of humankind, male and female, offer praise to God for Jesus.

Read Luke 2:21–35.

12. What brought Mary and Joseph to the temple?

13. Write down everything you can discover about Simeon. What was he like? Why was he at the temple? What had the Spirit revealed to him?

> *Simeon attained the desire of his heart, to see the Messiah. God allowed him to recognize the Messiah in Mary's arms. "It is right for those who are taking a very earnest interest in the cause of Christ to long to be allowed to accomplish a certain work for him."* 6
>
> W. Clarkson, *The Pulpit Commentary*

14. Do you long to accomplish a particular work for Christ? If so, what is it?

15. Here at the birth, only Simeon seems to have grasped the titanic struggle that will follow this baby. List at least four things which the Holy Spirit revealed to Simeon (Luke 2:34–35).

16. What do you think "so the thoughts of many hearts will be revealed" means?

*Jesus' ministry shows where hearts really are before God. Jesus will expose those who do not believe. He is a litmus test for the individual Jewish responses to the fulfillment of their promise. Do they believe or not? The reference to the heart points to the deepest seat of thought.*7

17. Later, after the Crucifixion and Resurrection, the Holy Spirit gave understanding to other disciples about the spiritual warfare surrounding Jesus.

    A. What did God reveal to Peter about this? (1 Peter 2:7–8)

    B. What did God reveal to John about this? (Rev. 12:1–5)

Philip Yancey says he has never seen the above verse from Revelation on a Christmas card.

> *In daily life two parallel histories occur simultaneously, one on earth and one in heaven. Revelation, however, views them together, allowing a quick look*

> *behind the scenes. On earth a baby was born, a king got wind of it, a chase ensued. In heaven the Great Invasion had begun, a daring raid by the ruler of the forces of good into the universe's seat of evil.* [8]

18. Tristine Rainier writes: "An experienced diarist … is willing to place questions in the diary and wait for answers." Put yourself in Mary's place as she listens to Simeon's prophecy. Write down some questions she might have placed in her diary.

At the end of her life, what might have been some of the answers to those questions?

Like Mary, we will experience sorrow in life for Jesus told us life is filled with trouble (John 16:33). And, if we are living godly lives, we will experience the same kind of spiritual battle that surrounded Jesus (2 Tim. 3:12).

19. Wise believers record questions in their journals concerning the sorrow they are experiencing or have experienced and then wait for the answers. What questions might you record?

Read Luke 2:36–38.

Anna's presence, Darrell Bock, explains, fits two key emphases of Luke. First, the focus on women who respond to Jesus. Second, the emphasis on rejoicing because of Jesus. She follows the pattern of Mary and Elizabeth, who were filled with joy because of the birth of the Savior.

Anna was a widow for a very long time, and she chose to remain a widow in order to fully serve God, a commendable action according to Scripture. One of the advantages of singleness for a believer is that she is more apt to learn to be truly dependent on God and to find that He indeed is sufficient (1 Cor. 7:25–40; 1 Tim. 5:5). Amy Carmichael, the single missionary to India whose journals have inspired so many, tells of the struggle she had in her youth as God asked her: "Am I not enough, My own—not enough for you?" Amy writes:

> *It was a long time before I could honestly answer, "Yes, You alone are enough for me." I remember the turmoil of soul I experienced before committing myself to follow Him on whatever path He would lead—remember as if it were yesterday. But at last—oh, the rest that came to me when I lifted my head and followed! For in acceptance there lies peace.*

Amy Carmichael, Candles in the Dark [9]

20. Observe what you can about Anna. In the ancient Near East, marriage occurred at age 13 or 14. About how long, would you surmise, had she been widowed? What had she been doing during those years?

21. Put yourself in Anna's shoes. Imagine her life, her feelings. What evidence do you find for Anna being a reflective person? How was she rewarded?

22. Have you discovered that God alone is enough for you—or are you still in the process of learning that? Share some ways God has been a "husband" to you in being a provider, protector, comforter, and confidante.

23. Are you in the habit of spending time alone with God in Scripture and in prayer on a daily basis? Anna also fasted. Fasting, as a spiritual discipline, is to encourage believers to spend time with God, to feast on spiritual bread. Have you experienced this benefit? If any of these are "habits" share when, where, and how you go about them.

DAY 4

Mary Treasured These Things in Her Heart

As in Luke 2:19, after the shepherd's visit, here again, in Luke 2:51, after listening to the amazing words of her twelve-year-old son, we are told: "His mother treasured all these things in her heart." She surely was a detective for the divine.

In a charming fictional book called *Mary's Journal*, Evelyn Bence says that while she knows that women of that day did not read or write, they did memorize God's Word and keep it in their hearts. And because Mary is repeatedly called a "ponderer," Evelyn says that "she is the kind of woman who, if alive today, would keep a journal."

Chuck Swindoll says: "Thoughts untangle themselves as they go down from the lips and through the fingertips." In my journal I record what God teaches me through His Word—and that helps me to be alert to His still small voice. I record my prayers and, subsequently, I highlight the answers to those prayers.

ACTION ASSIGNMENT

Your personal action assignment is to purchase a journal. I prefer a spiral-bound journal with a hardcover. Some prefer to keep their journal on their computer. There are advantages in each—but the important point is to keep one. I treasure the journal (The Hollow Tree) that my father left behind, filled with his favorite thoughts from the thousands of books he read. My husband Steve kept a prayer journal on his computer, and though I have purchased programs to help me crack the code, I have yet to succeed, and perhaps I am not supposed to! Dad's journal was for himself and for his descendants—and that has value. Steve's journal was for himself and God alone, and that also has value. Both were ponderers, and that made them men that stood apart from most men.

If you are not already keeping a journal, what kind will you keep? Where will you keep it?

In this journal, record some of your top remembrances from the first three chapters of Luke. What will you take away? How will you apply them?

Read Luke 2:41–52.

Evelyn Bence helps us to get in Mary's shoes, imagining the prayers and questions she might have recorded in her journal during this time:

> *Heaven be merciful. Jesus is gone. We've canvassed the whole caravan and no one has seen him since we broke up camp this morning. All day I've thought him with Joseph and the men ... Joseph assumed he, still a child after all, was with me and the women. ...*
>
> *Guilt: my utter lack of responsibility. I, given such a privileged charge, have let him—still a boy—slip out of my shelter. Will I find forgiveness for such gross negligence?*
>
> *... "Didn't you know I'd be here tending my Father's affairs?"*
>
> *Wait, go back to the angel's announcement of this coming child: "He will be called the Son of the Most High." ... Was Jesus saying something important to me?*
> Evelyn Bence, *Mary's Journal* [10]

24. Have you ever lost a child who was in your care? If so, what did you feel?

25. Gleaning from this passage, what phrases help you to know what Mary might have been feeling?

26. What questions do you imagine she might have put in her journal after this episode?

Review your memory verse.

Prayer Time

Give women an opportunity to share answers to the prayers they recorded on the card last week. Then ask for specific prayer requests and pray conversationally. The following diagram explains "popcorn prayer."

Close with the chorus from "O Come All Ye Faithful" (O Come Let Us Adore Him).

The Savior's Power

A squall came down on the lake,
so that the boat was being swamped,
and they were in great danger.

—Luke 8:23

The Savior's Power
(Luke 7—9)

He wasn't what they expected. He didn't hurl lightning bolts or float about the sky on a throne. Even John the Baptist, imprisoned, seems confused. He sent his disciples to Jesus to ask: "Are you the one who was to come, or should we expect someone else?" (Luke 7:20)

Philip Yancey *(The Jesus I Never Knew)* says that the Gospels read "like a 'Whodunit' (or as Alister McGrath has pointed out, a 'whowashe') detective story."[11] In Luke 7—9, the crowds keep asking: "Who is He?" He's obviously a V.I.P.—but who? When He heals a Gentile's servant, it seems He is a prophet. Then, when He raises a widow's only begotten son (told only in Luke), the people surmise He is in the *upper echelon* of prophets, like Elijah or Elisha, who also raised the dead. When Jesus forgives the sins of a repentant woman at the house of Simon, they ask: "Who is this who even forgives sins?" (Luke 7:49) When He stops the storm, the disciples say: "Who is this? He commands even the winds and the water, and they obey him" (Luke 8:25).

Who is He? A prophet? A great prophet? The Messiah? God Himself? In this oasis, you will see the majesty of His birth repeated in the majesty of His miracles. All this is leading to the climax of Luke, which is Peter's confession when Jesus asks him, "Who do you say I am?"

Peter answers: "The Christ of God" (Luke 9:20).

Fourth Stop!

Who Is This
Who Even Forgives Sins?

A significant theme in Luke is the universality of Christ's promises. All questions of social class, race, and gender break down. For example, Luke *alone* tells us about:

The shepherds (CHRIST CAME FOR THE POOR!)

The Good Samaritan (CHRIST CAME FOR THE OUTSIDER!)

Elizabeth, Anna, the grieving widow, Mary of Bethany sitting at His feet (CHRIST CAME FOR WOMEN!)

The religions of men discriminate against women. Many orthodox Jewish males prayed daily: "Thank You, God, I was not born a woman." But Jesus elevated women, obliterating worldly divisions. When the Pharisees shun the sinful woman who pours perfume on Jesus, Jesus rebukes their self-righteousness and asks, instead: "Will you come to Me in humble faith as this woman has?" If we do, Jesus tells us clearly, we are part of His family. The issue is not gender, nor class, nor race—but faith and obedience! "My mother and brothers are those who hear God's word and put it into practice" (Luke 8:21).

Prepare Your Heart to Hear

Before each of the following five devotional times, remember that it is not familiarity but obedience to God's truth that pleases Him.

Memory Work

Review your memory work from THE FIRST OASIS.

Then, for THE SECOND OASIS, you will be memorizing Luke 9:23–25. Begin this week with verse 23:

> *Then he said to them all: "If anyone would come after me, he must deny him-self and take up his cross daily and follow me."*

WARMUP

The crowds couldn't help but be amazed by Jesus. He was different—He responded to the faith of Gentiles and women! His miracles caused crowds to follow Him. But soon they discovered His teachings were hard, the cost of discipleship high. Offended, they began to fall away. In the climax of chapter 7, Jesus says: "Blessed is he who is not off-ended because of Me" (v. 23, NKJV). Name a teaching of our Lord which offends the world or which you struggle to completely obey.

DAY I

Overview

Read Luke 7—8.

1. Read all of the introductory notes. Comment on what stood out to you from:
   A. The introductory notes for THE SECOND OASIS: The Savior's Power (p. 37)
   B. The introductory notes for The Fourth Stop! Who Is This Who Even Forgives Sins? (p. 38)
2. Read Luke 7 as an overview. Trace the escalating mystery concerning the identity of Jesus. What were some of the things he said and did that might have shocked those listening?

Spend five minutes on the memory passages.

Journal Entry: Spend three minutes entering a few remarks in your journal on what God impressed on your heart.

DAY 2

He Responds to Outsiders!

Sometimes I am amazed when I meet a spiritual giant and then discover he did not have the advantage of a Christian home. I think that is the way Jesus felt when He met the cen-turion, a Gentile whose faith surpassed the faith of Jesus' own Jewish disciples. The cen-turion had not witnessed the miracles of Jesus firsthand, nor did he ask to touch Jesus. Instead, he sent two delegations to Jesus, asking Jesus to heal his beloved slave from a distance. A man of power who commanded thousands in the Roman army, the centurion was still a humble man, saying he was unworthy to have Jesus come to his house. The Jews respected him, saying he had built their synagogue. (The ruins of a white marble synagogue still stand in Capernaum.) The centurion's military mind uses an army analogy, saying that Jesus had authority over thousands of angels!

Read Luke 7:1–10.

3. Be a detective by asking yourself relentless questions. Who was this centurion—what can you discover about his character, feelings, reputation, etc?

4. Though the centurion was a Gentile—a man of a different race—Jesus responded to him and commended his faith. Jesus came not only to the poor, but also to the outsider. This impartiality is a central message in Luke, one which he heard Paul proclaim repeatedly as he traveled with him. How do the following teachings of Paul explain or elaborate on the impartiality of Christ's promises to those who believe?

   A. Galatians 3:7–9

   B. Galatians 3:28–29

   C. Ephesians 2:8–20

5. Satan longs for us to be divided in our homes, in our churches, and in the Body of Christ. He wants us to be prejudiced, to judge each other on the basis of race, class, gender, or denomination! One of the beautiful aspects of the story of the centurion was to see how the Jews and Gentiles loved and respected each other as they shared faith in God. What do you learn from the following passages about the importance of love and unity?

   A. 1 Corinthians 1:1–13

   B. 1 Corinthians 3:3–9

   C. John 17:20–23

In John 17:20–23, Jesus' last prayer before the cross was for us, that we as believers would love each other. Why? So that the world will believe Christianity is true.

> *We cannot expect the world to believe that the Father sent the Son, that Jesus' claims are true, and that Christianity is true, unless the world sees some reality of the oneness of true Christians.*
>
> Francis Schaeffer, *The Church at the End of the Twentieth Century* [12]

Review your memory work.

Personal Action Assignment

6. Are you aware of any division between you and a member of the Body of Christ? What could you do to increase peace between you?

7. Do you, like the centurion, believe that Jesus can intervene and answer prayer? If so, come to Him now in fervent intercessory prayer. Record your requests here or in your journal.

DAY 3

He Must Be in the Upper Echelon of Prophets!

Now we move to another "woman's story" told only in Luke. (See one artist's rendition on p. 7.) Jesus amazes the crowd by stopping a funeral procession. Moved with compassion by seeing the "only son" of a widow carried out, Jesus touches the dead man and commands him, as He will do again with Lazarus, to rise! Abruptly the son sat up and "Jesus gave him back to his mother." The crowd is "seized with fear" and reassesses their opinion of Jesus. The only prophets who have raised the dead were the cream of the cream: Elijah and Elisha. Jesus is not only a prophet—He is a "great prophet!"

8. Meditate on Luke 7:11–17. Be a detective! (Who, when, how, what, why...)

What do you see?

9. Read the story again.

   A. Even the word "widow" has a connotation of sorrow. If you are a widow, share something of the sorrow of widowhood. If you are not, try to imagine what would be some of the things you would miss.

   B. Luke often uses the phrase "only son." What do you make of this?

   C. What phrase describes the motive for raising the widow's son?

According to Numbers 19:11, it was an act of defilement to touch a coffin. Darrell Bock

41

writes: "Cleanliness is next to godliness except where compassion is required." Bock also says that Jesus may have touched the coffin to get the pallbearers to stop. [13]

   D. Whom does Jesus address in Luke 7:14? Why would this be humorous or tragic if it were not Jesus?

   E. What comfort does this story give you?

Personal Reflection Only

Is there a heartache or concern in your life which you have been carrying alone? Sing "Turn Your Eyes Upon Jesus" from your hymnal. As you sing, put your burden in the strong arms of Jesus.

10. Imagine that someone comes across your path (or your mind) who is hurting, lonely, or lost today? How, according to the above passage, do you think Jesus would respond? How, according to 1 John 3:14–18, should you?

Personal Action Assignment

Ask the Lord to open your eyes and to give you compassion for someone in need in your life. Then ask the Lord to show you a specific way to respond and do it. (You will tell one person in the group next week what you did.)

Review your memory verse.

11. What is the response of the crowd to the raising of this young man from the dead?

Why do you think fear often follows miracles in the New Testament?

How do you think you would feel if the raising of the young man happened today?

DAY 4

But Is He the Messiah?

In this key section, John the Baptist, who has been imprisoned for confronting Herod about his adulterous affair, sends his disciples to Jesus to ask: "Are you the one who was to come, or should we expect someone else?" (Luke 7:19)

Doesn't John know Jesus is the Messiah? Is John using the Socratic method, asking a question so that Jesus can clarify to the crowds who He is? Possibly, though it would be understandable if John himself had questions. He is in prison for doing what was right and Jesus is not miraculously releasing him. Why not? Is Jesus truly the Messiah?

Jesus answers John by showing that He has been fulfilling Isaiah's prophecies concerning the Messiah. And then Jesus gives a gentle rebuke: "And blessed is he, whosoever shall not be offended in me" (Luke 7:23, KJV).

We need to take these words to heart. The words of Jesus are still offending people—and even believers have trouble trusting wholeheartedly. Jesus asks us to put Him first in our lives, even over our devotion to husbands, children, and parents (Luke 14:26). He asks us to look for reward in the spiritual rather than the material (Matt. 6:33). He asks us to deny ourselves, to lose ourselves completely in Him! (Luke 9:23) These are hard sayings, but Jesus says that if we are not offended by them, and instead embrace them wholly, we will be greatly blessed.

Certainly many secular women today are offended by the idea that women should wait until marriage for sexual intimacy, should be in submission to their husbands, and should stay married for life. Likewise, people scoff at the idea of hell, yet Jesus teaches clearly about it (Luke 12:5). The reason God sent Jesus to die on a cross was to pay the price for our sin and to save anyone who would believe from the fires of hell. The message of the cross is foolishness to those who are perishing (1 Cor. 1:18). Simeon prophesied that the coming of the Christ would reveal the hearts of many, and would be a divisive message.

How do you respond to Jesus? If you believe that He is, indeed, the Messiah, then will you embrace and obey His radical teachings? If you do, you will indeed be blessed!

Review your memory passage.

Read Luke 7:18–23.

12. How does Jesus respond to John the Baptist's question?

13. Explain how His response shows a fulfillment of messianic prophecy:

    A. Isaiah 26:19

    B. Isaiah 29:18–19

    C. Isaiah 35:5–6

    D. Isaiah 61:1

14. Jesus continues in Luke with hard teachings. Summarize the hard teaching in each of the following passages and then answer: "How am I truly responding to this teaching?"

    A. Luke 9:23–25

    B. Luke 12:4–5

    C. Luke 12:15

    D. Luke 12:27–31

Read Luke 7:27–35.

15. How does Jesus commend the character of John the Baptist in verse 28?

16. What have you seen in John the Baptist that was worthy of praise? (See Luke 3:7–9, 15–16, 19.)

17. Jesus then condemns the Pharisees who were offended by John and now by Jesus. They claimed to be offended by the lifestyle of both of them, but in reality, they were offended by the hard message of repentance and faith. How does Jesus show this in Luke 7:31–35?

When Jesus compares the people to children in 7:31–32, He is saying: Unless you can make the rules to the game, you don't want to play. To many it seems more attractive to make up their own religion than to follow the hard teachings of Jesus.

Personal Action Assignment

Are you offended by Jesus' hard sayings? If not, and you desire to embrace Him wholeheartedly, how should you live today? Be still before the Lord. Journal what He impresses on your heart. Then *walk* in the Spirit!

DAY 5
....

Who But God Can Forgive Sins?

Imagine the scene. A dinner party at a fine home. A woman with an immoral past shocks the guests by entering, falling on her knees before Jesus, and pouring an expensive jar of perfume on His feet. It took great courage for her to come, but she was compelled by gratefulness. Then, adding one shock to another, this "prophet" tells her that her sins are forgiven! The nerve! Who does this man think He is? After all, who has the authority to forgive sins but God alone? (This incident, another "woman's incident," is found only in Luke. Many do not realize this, confusing this incident with a different incident involving the devout Mary of Bethany, which we will study in The Third Oasis. Many also have also confused this woman with Mary Magdalene, but there is neither scriptural nor historical basis for that.) The message in this incident is that repentance and faith are necessary for salvation. In fact, that is all that is necessary! Dr. Darrell Bock told me: "There is a marvelous lesson here for those with a lurid past. This message of forgiveness for *any-one* is Luke's emphasis." The Pharisees reject this message, and attack the messenger (Luke 7:33–35). So Jesus then turns to His host, Simon the Pharisee, and says, in words that would have stopped my heart, "Simon, I have something to tell you" (Luke 7:40).

Read Luke 7:36–50.

18. Make observations, asking who, when, what, why, and how.

19. Contrast the heart of Simon with the heart of the sinful woman. Give Scripture references to support your answer.

    The woman   *Simon the Pharisee*

20. How does Jesus help Simon to understand the difference between his heart and the heart of the woman?

At the age of 21, I was confronted with the claims of Christ. The more I examined Jesus, much as the people are doing in Luke 7, the more in awe I grew. Could it be? Could this Man who came to earth actually be God? Was His death on the cross a purposeful choice to pay for my sin? And when He said that He was the only way to heaven, was He telling the truth?

I remember the November day I fell on my knees and surrendered my life to Christ. At that moment, God's Holy Spirit opened my eyes to three things, in rapid succession:

1. The profound holiness of God

2. My own wretched sinfulness

3. God's amazing grace in washing me of my sin

And I, like this sinful woman in Luke 7, wept in gratitude. Then, more than anything, I wanted to live fully for Christ! If you have never wept for your sin, if you have never been overwhelmed with gratitude toward Jesus, perhaps you have yet to realize who Jesus is and what He did for you.

21. Has there ever been a time when you, like the sinful woman in Luke, wept for your sin? If so, share something about your feelings at the time.

22. Have there also been times when, like Simon the Pharisee, you lacked gratitude and an awareness of all Jesus is and is giving you? If so, how can you increase your thankfulness?

Sing "Amazing Grace" in your personal devotional time as a way of praising God.

23. What evidence is there in your life that you are profoundly thankful to Jesus?

Read Luke 8:1–3.

24. What do you learn about the women who traveled with Jesus?

These women had experienced the power of Jesus in their lives and now were helping to support Him. It is likely that they were one of Luke's sources of information. Dr. Darrell Bock tells us the following about them:

> An itinerant ministry like Jesus' was common, and support from women was common; but it was unusual for women to travel with a rabbi. The first woman, Mary Magdalene, was freed from the presence of seven demons...She was not the sinful woman who anointed Jesus. Nor is it clear that she was immoral... Mary stayed faithful to Jesus, for it is recorded that she watched the Crucifixion, saw where Jesus was laid, and participated in the anointing of the body...The mention of Joanna who also is present with Mary Magdalene in Luke 24:10, indicates the scope of Jesus' ministry. Jesus' message had reached into the world of the powerful, for Joanna was the wife of Chuza, who served as an administrative official in Herod's court...The third woman, Susanna, is mentioned only here...[14]

25. If time permits, have women share the lesson God impressed on their hearts through this study.

Prayer Time

Instead of sharing individual prayer requests, have each woman lift her own request up in prayer. Then have a few women support her with sentences. When there is a silence, another woman should lift up her individual prayer request. Close with a familiar chorus such as "God Is So Good."

Fifth Stop!

Who Is This
Who Stops Storms?

The disciples have seen Jesus do miracles that only the greatest of prophets have done. Recently they saw Him claim to forgive sins. Their minds are swirling.

Now two things happen that escalate the drama. Up to now the miracles of Jesus have impacted others. Now the disciples themselves are the recipients. Also, up to now the miracles of Jesus had also been performed by the greatest of prophets. Now He does something that has never been done. He stops a raging storm on the sea. Imagine the scene.

Fishermen say the storms on the Sea of Galilee are formidable. With Jesus asleep in the boat, the disciples are overcome by fear as lightning crashes next to them and waves swamp the boat. They cry out to Jesus in terror. I am not sure what they expected Him to do, but what He does do astonishes them. He stands and rebukes the wind and the raging waters. Immediately all is calm. The disciples look at one another in fear—for now they feared the POWER of the One who stopped the storm even more than the storm. "Who is this? He commands even the wind and the water, and they obey him" (Luke 8:25).

Prepare Your Heart to Hear

Before each of the following five devotional times, quiet your heart and ask God to speak to you personally from His Word. He has the POWER to do it!

47

Memory Work

Complete your memorization of Luke 9:23–25.

> *Then he said to them all: "If anyone would come after me, he must deny him-*
> *self and take up his cross daily and follow me. For whoever wants to save his*
> *life will lose it, but whoever loses his life for me will save it. What good is it for*
> *a man to gain the whole world, and yet lose or forfeit his very self?"*

(When you share your memory work do it in pairs. Also, share if you prayed about show-ing compassion to someone and if you acted on it. Be honest! If you didn't do either your memory work or your accountability assignment, forgive yourself—but do your memo-ry work at THE THIRD OASIS.)

WARMUP

Recall some of the times you have *personally* been impacted by the POWER of Jesus: in stopping a storm in your life, in delivering you from fear, or in providing for you. Share one briefly and how it affected your faith in Christ.

DAY I
. . . .

Overview

Read Luke 9-10.

1. Read the introduction for The Fifth Stop! Who Is This Who Stops Storms? (p. 47) and write a summary sentence.

2. Luke wants us to understand God's power. What does it accomplish in each of the fol-lowing verses?

    A. Luke 1:35

    B. Luke 4:36

    C. Luke 5:17

    D. Luke 12:5

    E. Luke 21:27

3. Leading up to the story of Jesus stopping the storm are three exhortations to faith. Briefly explain:

   A. How the parable of the sower (Luke 8:1–15) contrasts ineffective and effective faith in the Savior's power.

   B. How a "hidden light" is a picture of ineffective faith in the Savior's power (Luke 8:16–18).

   C. How Jesus describes his true family (Luke 8:19–21).

Spend five minutes on the memory passage.

Briefly journal what God impressed on your heart today.

DAY 2

Power over Nature and Demons

Our daughter Sally tells of the storm that came into her life and, consequently, ours, when we adopted Annie, an absolutely adorable five-year-old from an orphanage in Korea:

> *Until then I'd been the only girl and my parents and brothers lavished attention on me. Suddenly the spotlight turned from me to her, and I felt unloved. I also felt huge and awkward next to this petite little doll. Though I'd been excited about having a sister, I didn't like her. I didn't want to play with her, talk to her, or be in the same room with her. Everything she did bugged me—even her breathing.*

Our sunny Sally soon was exhibiting the signs of a full-blown depression. She wasn't sleeping at night, she was losing weight, and she was overwhelmed by sadness. And Annie was hurt by Sally's rejection. One morning during my quiet time I cried out to the Lord, much like the disciples cried out to Jesus during their storm: "O Lord—I thought You led us to adopt Annie—but I feel like our ship is going down!" Engulfed in self-pity, tears ran down my cheeks. "Lord, help us!"

My husband, strong in the Lord and a physician acquainted with depression, said: "I think Sally may be suffering from depression and I want to have her tested for a chemical imbalance. But I also realize there is a spiritual problem here, so we need to pray that she will recognize that."

Tests did reveal a chemical imbalance in Sally and, after she had been on medication for a month, we saw a real change in her. She was sleeping, eating, and even smiling. Sally says:

> *I felt good enough to go out again. I went to a Christian concert that stirred me deeply. At the closing I went up and knelt at the altar, praying: "Lord, I know I am supposed to love my new sister, but I don't. You know the yuk and jealousy that have been in my heart. O Lord, I am so sorry—but I need Your help. I can't seem to do this on my own. Please take away the yuk and fill me with love for Annie."*

Amazingly, God did exactly that. He bent down and listened to that eleven-year-old's cry and filled her with love for her sister. He stopped the storm in our family. The sun came out for Sally, for us, and for little Annie, who, like a drooping flower, began to brighten.

Read Luke 8:22–25.

4. Describe the miracle. (Remember: who, what, where, how, why)

    A. Put yourself in the boat. Describe your thoughts and feelings.

    B. Why do you think they feared Jesus after the storm was calmed?

5. What rebuke does Jesus give to the disciples?

6. A. In the midst of pressure, what are some things we should remember about God which will help us to trust?

    B. Is there an application to your life right now? If so, what?

7. A popular Christian song has the lyrics: "Sometimes He calms the storm—and sometimes He calms His child." Share a time when the storm was not stopped—yet God gave you His peace.

8. Describe the power Jesus displayed in Luke 8:26–39.

Spend time reviewing your memory passage and write a few sentences in your journal.

DAY 3
. . . .

Power over Death and Disease

On the way to raise a little girl from death, another miracle occurs, the healing of a a woman who, for 12 years, had suffered the embarrassment of bleeding, a woman's ailment when something is amiss with the menstrual cycle. She was unclean. Shunned. She had spent all she had at the hands of physicians—and only grew worse. (Mark tells us this detail. Luke, the physician, omits it!) Ken Gire, in *Intimate Moments with the Savior*, gives us this portrait:

> *She is destitute now. And being out of money, the doctors finally admit there is nothing they can do for her. Her life is ebbing away. The steady loss of blood over the years has taken its toll. She is anemic, pale, and tired. So very, very tired...*
>
> *She no longer dreams of marriage and a family...of combing the hair of a daughter...of bouncing a grandbaby on her knee....Her suffering has whisked those dreams into little broken piles.*
>
> *But stories of another physician reach down to pick up the pieces of those dreams. A physician who charges no fee...Who comes not to the strong but to the downtrodden..."if I can find this Jesus and but touch the fringe of his garment..."[15]*

This particular miracle made a deep impression on the later church, for as the story was repeated down through the centuries, the woman was given the name Bernice.[16]

Read Luke 8:40–56.

9. Describe this miracle that "interrupted" the journey to Jairus' daughter. Make observations.

10. The woman's emotions must have been strong. Put yourself in her shoes and imagine how you would feel and why at each of these times:

    A. Mark 5:25–26

    B. Mark 5:27–28

    C. Mark 5:29

    D. Luke 8:45

    E. Luke 8:46

    F. Luke 8:47

In order for the woman to have been accepted back into society, the cure needed to be made public, and Jesus is careful, in verse 47, to arrange this.

G. Luke 8:48

This is the only time in the New Testament Jesus calls someone "daughter". He is pleased with her faith. She is an example also of courageously testifying to the world of the power of God. May we be like her!

11. How do you think Jairus was feeling during this interruption? What does the messenger tell him in Luke 8:49?

12. Have you ever been at a deathbed and seen the spirit of a person leave? Describe it. What, according to Luke 8:55, happened to the daughter of Jairus?

DAY 4

Power to Provide for Your Every Need

When my husband and I were young, poor, and new in the faith, a missionary asked us to pray about helping to provide her way to Africa. We prayed about it and decided to give her 50 dollars—which seemed like a lot to us. However, when my husband wrote the check, instead of 50 dollars, he wrote out more than 12 times that amount, erroneously writing out the balance in our checkbook! And then he mailed it, oblivious to his error.

Weeks later we received a letter from Africa in which the missionary told us she had wept when she received our check with the exact amount, to the penny, of what she needed. God had moved Steve's hand, though she thought He had moved his heart!

It was only when we read her letter that Steve realized his mistake. Amazingly, none of the checks we had written since then had bounced. And though our balance was tiny, God provided for us over the next few months. A small inheritance check. A gift from friends. Groceries that somehow seemed to stretch.

Is God still in the business of multiplying? Yes, He is! He has the creativity and the *power* to provide when we trust Him.

Read Luke 9:1–17.

13. Why do you think Jesus send out the disciples with so few provisions?

14. The basic lesson of this miracle is also taught by Jesus in Matthew 6:31–33. What is it and how can you apply this, right now, to your life?

15. There is also an important lesson for ministry. What did the disciples learn and how could you apply this to ministries to which God has called you?

The most fruitful women's ministries I have known are those which begin by seeking God's idea rather than coming up with their own idea and then asking God to bless it. When we step into what God is already doing, it is like stepping into a raging river, and we experience POWER!

16. If you have had the experience of stepping into God's power in ministry, share something about it.

17. What can you learn from Jesus' model of teaching in the miracle of feeding the 5,000?

Child Evangelism Fellowship encourages teachers to act out Bible stories and their lessons with children for they have found: "Children forget what they hear, they remember what they see, and they understand what they do." The disciples surely remembered this miracle—it is recorded in all four Gospels.

18. As a mother, or teacher of children, how could you follow the teaching example of Jesus in Luke 9:10–17?

Choose *one* of the following miracles and brainstorm ways you could teach it so that children would understand the main principle *and* how to apply it to their lives:

■ The feeding of the multitudes

■ The stopping of the storm

DAY 5
But Who Do You Say That I Am?

We have reached the climax and a turning point in Luke. The question is finally articulated. Jesus asks first: "Who do the crowds say I am?" The speculation is that Jesus is from God, yet the crowds have no idea that Jesus *is* God Incarnate. But do the disciples understand? Jesus turns to Peter, asking him to speak for the men: "But what about you? Who do you say I am?" Peter's reply to this crucial question brings to our mind the regal opening of Luke: the angels, Simeon, Anna—all announcing that this is the Messiah, the Savior, *Christ the Lord.*

Read Luke 9:18–20.

19. What are the people saying? Who do they think Jesus is?

20. There was a popular belief that a prophet of the past would reappear just before the Messiah came. What similarities might they have noticed between Elijah and Jesus? (See 1 Kings 17:10–24) Why would John the Baptist be on their minds? (Luke 9:9)

21. How does Peter answer the question of Jesus?

22. In Luke 9:21–22, what prophecy does Jesus make that will soon be fulfilled?

23. What hard teaching does Jesus give in Luke 9:23–26? What does He mean?

When my sister lifted up the claims of Christ to me, she said: "Jesus wants you to give Him your whole life."

I responded, "Does this mean that I will have to give up the expensive house Steve and I are planning to build?"

Courageously, my sister said: "It seems to me that you think that house will fill up the emptiness in your life—and only God can do that. Therefore, I think this house is like a god to you and will have to go."

I hesitated. My sister said: "But it will be worth it, Dee. Jesus said that if you try to hold onto your life, you will lose it—but if you give it up for Him, you will find it again. And what does it profit you if you gain the world, including that beautiful house, and lose your soul?"

My sister was absolutely right. And I have often said similar words to a person who is wavering between the broad and the narrow road. One woman asked me: "If I gave my life to Jesus, would I have to stop living with my boyfriend?" I answered much as my sister answered me.

This truth applies not only in salvation, but on a daily basis in living for Christ. No cross—no crown. No discipline—no harvest of righteousness. Whether the discipline involves saying no to the flesh, no to an abortion, no to a dishonest monetary gain, or no to the fears that keep us from being a witness for Christ—so often the wrong choice seems easy at first, but leads to regret—and the right choice seems hard at first but leads to joy and peace.

Share the memory passage and your reflections on it.

24. Be still before the Lord and ask Him to show you how to apply the truth articulated in this verse in your life right now.

25. What particularly stood out to you from the above section?

Prayer Time

In conversational prayer, lift up your own answer to question 24 audibly and allow two or three other women to say sentence prayers asking God for His help to obey in this area. When there is a pause, another woman should lift up her answer to question 24.

Close with a familiar chorus like "He Is Lord."

The Savior's Wisdom

She had a sister, Mary,
who sat before the Master,
hanging on every word he said.

—Luke 10:39 The Message

The Savior's Wisdom
(Luke 10–12; 15)

With Luke 10, the Gospel shifts to "the Jerusalem journey." Jesus begins to teach His disciples intensely, knowing the end is near, and those disciples include women. We will begin this oasis with a careful look at Mary and Martha of Bethany.

Luke *alone* records the incident that occurs in the home of Mary and Martha. Martha is upset that Mary is not helping her in the kitchen. But instead of rebuking Mary, instead of brushing her into the kitchen, Jesus firmly protects her, saying, "Mary has chosen what is better, and it will not be taken away from her" (Luke 10:42).

Only men were to sit at the feet of a rabbi (the women were to learn at home from their men)! Jesus is revolutionary in the way He treats women, turning upside down the accepted attitude toward women. His attitude was different from the disciples, different from His contemporaries, different, even, from the attitude of many Christians today toward women. Dorothy Sayers put it like this: "A teacher who never nagged at them, who never flattered or coaxed or patronized; who never made arch jokes about them ... who took their questions and arguments seriously." [17]

Jesus certainly took Mary of Bethany seriously, and she Him. Should we not learn from this unusual woman?

For the next four weeks, as you journey through His wisdom, diligently practice Mary's habit of sitting at His feet on a daily basis. Choose the same place and the same time each day—strive to listen, not just to complete your daily assignment. This WISDOM OASIS is filled with practical teachings on priorities, prayer, and parables! God has something of immense value for you personally, each day. Don't miss it! Jesus tells us: "He who has ears to hear, let him hear" (Luke 14:35).

Sixth Stop!

Mary of Bethany

John (John 11:5) mentions that Jesus loved these three siblings: Mary, Martha, and Lazarus. The evidence is strong that they were some of His closest friends and that He visited them often, particularly now, as He is honing in on Jerusalem, for Bethany was an easy walk (less than two miles) from the Holy City. I like to think that the One who had no home and "no place to lay His head" (Luke 9:58) found some comfort here. In order to see the whole picture we will begin in Luke, but then travel to the Gospel of John.

I have known a few women like Mary of Bethany. My older sister Sally always begins her day in hours of prayer and study and then asks: "Lord, this is Your day. Your plans are best. How would You have me spend it?" Because of her listening heart, God has given her incredible wisdom and timing. She knew exactly the right time, 40 years ago, to visit me and lift up the claims of Christ. God used Sally's visit to bring me and my husband to the Savior. Sally has prayed her family, one by one, into the Kingdom. Each day, she earnestly seeks Jesus. For this reason I dedicated this guide about the Savior to my sister Sally.

Almost 30 years ago my husband and I asked God, unless He had a better idea, to give us a daughter who had a spiritually tender heart like that of her Aunt Sally, like that of Mary of Bethany! God graciously answered our prayers, and we named her Sally. Even as a little girl our daughter thirsted for God. The psalmist says that the "secret of the LORD is with those who fear Him" (Ps. 25:14 NKJV). The Lord reveals "secrets" to the "Mary of Bethany" kind of seekers. You will learn what He showed Mary. Our daughter Sally was pondering the problem of suffering—and the Lord revealed a secret to her. She was painting Aslan the lion who represents Jesus from C. S. Lewis's *The Lion, The Witch, and The Wardrobe*. Lewis writes that Aslan is "not safe, but he is good." Sally was trying to capture this paradox, asking the Lord to direct her hands as she painted. She felt she had captured the "not safe" part in the ferocity of the lion—"But where," she asked God, "is the good part?" To her amazement, when she completed the painting, we all saw another animal in the painting. Clearly, near the heart of the lion, was a lamb who looked as if he had been slain. (See the painting and watch a video clip on my Web site of Sally telling this story. My Web site is DeeBrestin.com) God revealed a mystery to Sally as she sought Him. He certainly is not safe, for on the day Sally completed Aslan her dad was diagnosed with fourth stage colon cancer. Yet, He is good. He is the lamb who was slain for us. So though there is enormous pain in this world, He loves us, and in His time, He will do all things well.

Don't you long for a Mary of Bethany heart? Don't you long for God to "confide His secrets" in you? Let's take a good look at this woman to whom Luke first introduces us.

Prepare Your Heart to Hear

Each day, choose to sit at Jesus' feet, asking Him to help you hear "your portion" for the day.

Memory Work

This week learn Luke 10:41–42.

> *"Martha, Martha," the Lord answered, "you are worried and upset about many things, but only one thing is needed. Mary has chosen what is better, and it will not be taken away from her."*

WARMUP

Overcoming distractions is a common problem for women who tend to have many roles. What kind of things typically distract you, keeping you from sitting at the Lord's feet and listening?

DAY I

. . . .

Overview

Read Luke 11—12.

1. Read all of the introductory notes. Comment on what stood out to you from:

   A. The introductory notes for THE THIRD OASIS: The Savior's Wisdom (p. 57)

   B. The introductory notes for The Sixth Stop! Mary of Bethany (p. 58)

Spend five minutes on the memory passage.

In your personal quiet time sing: "As the Deer" or "Breathe on Me, Breath of God" from your hymnal.

Read Luke 10:38–42

2. A. Record your observations on WHO (Look carefully at exactly who came to the home of Mary and Martha—was it all the disciples or just Jesus? Who seemed to be the hostess? Other WHO questions?)

B. Record your observations on WHERE (Use cross-references to discover the name of the village. Look at a Bible map to see what city it was near. Where was Martha? Mary? Other WHERE questions?)

C. Record your observations on WHAT (What was each person doing? What happened? What was said? What did Jesus mean by "only one thing is needed"? Other WHAT questions?)

D. Record your observations on HOW. (How do you think each person was feeling? Other HOW questions?)

E. Record your observations on WHY. (Why did God include this story? Why did Jesus rebuke a woman who was serving him? Why did He protect Mary?)

Did your questions give you any new insights? If so, what are they?

DAY 2
One Thing Is Needed

Walter Wangerin in *The Book of God, The Bible as a Novel*, helps us imagine the story as it could have happened. Mary is reflecting:

> *Jesus will sometimes find lodging with us. He arrives unannounced, often in the middle of the night. We rise up in the morning and find him sitting in our courtyard*

under the grape arbor, resting. He says he rests best sitting up.

My sister is immediately delighted to see him. "Well!" she says, clapping her hands and causing every soft part of her body to wobble: "Well, then! We must make cakes!"

During these last three years he has usually come in the company of his disciples. He first makes sure that they all have food and places to sleep in Bethany, then he slips silently into our courtyard.[18]

I found Wangerin's imagination intriguing. I certainly could imagine a well-rounded Martha, fond of putting on a good spread. The idea that Jesus came alone to their home was also interesting, for I used to think: *Poor Martha. Alone in the kitchen, fixing lunch for 13 men, and when she asks for help, she gets a rebuke!*

Was she, indeed, fixing lunch for only one man? I looked again—the pronouns in Luke 10:38 indeed imply that Jesus was alone. If Jesus was alone, I thought, *What was all the hubbub about?* I laughed to hear Chuck Swindoll say, "Martha, Martha—chips and dip would be fine."

Suddenly a different picture began to appear, a more accurate one. I began to understand the rebuke of Jesus.

Central to understanding this story is to glean what it was that Martha had missed and what it was that Mary had chosen. What is "the only one thing needed," "the most important thing," "the better part"?

The story of Mary and Martha is the middle episode of three passages that examine our relationship with God and with others. Therefore, it is important to look back at the first episode, and see how it begins.

3. A lawyer comes to Jesus in Luke 10:25. He asks Jesus a question. What is it?

4. Jesus responds with a question. What is it?

5. Jesus has asked the lawyer, in essence, "What is the most important thing in the law?" The lawyer responds with the *Shema* from Deuteronomy 6:4: "Hear, O Israel The LORD our God, the LORD is one! You shall love the LORD your God with all your heart, with all your soul, and with all your strength," and with Leviticus 19:18: "...love your neighbor as yourself." How does Jesus respond to this answer in Luke 10:28?

The *Shema* was recited twice a day by practicing first-century Jews, and faithful Jews still recite it. These two laws, of loving God and loving our neighbor appear throughout the law. In fact, the Ten Commandments are divided into these two categories.

6. A similar interchange between Jesus and an expert in the law is recorded in Matthew

22:34–40. Here Jesus replies directly. What is the question and what is the answer?

7. In Revelation, Jesus has a word for seven different churches. He offers them constructive criticism, with words of commendation and rebuke. Look at the church in Ephesus in Revelation 2:1–7. What good things does Jesus see in the church? But what most important thing does he hold against them?

The NAS translates the rebuke of Jesus to Martha in Luke 10:42 as: "*Only* a few things are necessary, really *only* one, for Mary has chosen the good part, which shall not be taken away from her." This rebuke is similar to the rebuke to Ephesus.

8. Scripture is its own best commentary and interpreter. As you look over the above passages, what would you say is the most important thing that is required of us?

9. Now, read again the words of Jesus to Martha in Luke 10:41–42. What does He say? Why, do you think, He is rebuking her and commending and protecting Mary?

So often I have heard people defend Martha, saying, "We need Marthas." It is true that there are different temperaments. There are those who are naturally physically busy and those who are naturally more sedate and reflective. Yet every single one of us needs to remember the most important thing: *to love the Lord fervently.* When we do that, service will come as well, but it *will* be service that is directed by God and that glorifies God.

Complete your memory work.

DAY 3

In Quietness and Confidence Shall Be Your Strength

Amy Shreve-Wixtrom reminds me of Mary of Bethany. Even though she performs before thousands, Amy is actually an introvert, drawing strength from time alone, sitting at the feet of Jesus. Read carefully Amy's lyrics to "Martha's Song":

Martha's Song

Amy Shreve-Wixtrom

With a million things expecting His attention
Jesus took the time to meet us in our home
There were so many people here to ask Him questions
And my sister, Mary, left me all the work to do alone

Well, I've always been responsible and helpful
Mary just gets lost in what she wants to see
But when I complained of her unwillingness to help me
Jesus said she chose the better part,
simply sitting at His feet

Just to be closer to Jesus
Just to be near His sweet voice
To bask in His presence my cares all fade into joy
Just to be closer to Jesus
Receiving the peace He imparts
I want to want most of all
Just to be near His heart.

With a million things demanding my attention
I realize now that Mary knew a precious thing
There's no accomplishment or praise that can compare to
Leaving all my worries far behind & simply worshiping my King.

10. Find everything you can in Luke 10:38–42 that describes the sisters and helps us to see the contrast between them.

               Martha   Mary

Review your memory verse. The word that J.B. Phillips paraphrases "bothered" in Luke 10:41 is also translated "upset or troubled." It comes from the Greek word *turbazo* (emotionally stirred up). Our words "tumultuous" and "turbulent" come from this Greek word.

11. What images or word pictures do the words "tumultuous" or "turbulent" bring to your mind?

12. If we fail to listen to the Lord, "sitting at His feet," hearing from Him, we may actually be working at cross-purposes with Him, though it seems like we are serving Him. How was this true of Martha in the Luke passage?

One woman said: "When I sit down with the Lord, Satan whispers: 'Just put a load of wash in.' So, I hop up and put a load of wash in. Then I sit down and he will whisper: 'Just clear the dishes.' Then the phone rings and somehow, I never get back to the Lord. Now I recognize the enemy's voice and shut him out. God is first in my life, so I get up before the children and spend time with Him. He comes before housework, before reading the paper, before anything!"

13. If you have learned some methods which help you overcome distractions in your prayer or Bible study time, please share.

14. What do you learn from the following Scriptures?
    A. Psalm 46:10

    B. Ecclesiastes 4:6

    C. Isaiah 30:15

    D. Psalm 131:1–2

Dr. S. Conway has given me insight into the imagery of "a child weaned from its mother." A loving mother gently weans her child from the breast to the cup. Though he loved the breast, in time, the very desire for the breast is gone—he is happy and content. Likewise, God longs to wean us from the world, to help us to be content with what He has for us.[19]

15. How does the word picture from Psalm 131 of "stilling and quieting your soul like a weaned child with its mother" speak to you?

16. A. From what might you need to be weaned in order to have time for the Lord?

    B. How do you go about quieting yourself when you meet with God?

    C. From what might you need to be weaned to live wholeheartedly for Christ?

17. According to 1 Timothy 2:1–3, what kind of lives please God our Savior?

18. When you look at the above standard, assess your life honestly.

Not only do many adults fail to live quiet and peaceful lives, but the lifestyle of children has radically changed. "Being a kid," *USA Today* reports in a front page article on July 12, 2005, "isn't what it used to be." In the ten years between 1995 and 2005, kids are moving "indoors." Fishing, biking, spontaneous games of baseball, and swimming have decreased by nearly 20%. A child is six times as likely to play a video game as to ride a bike on any given day.[20] Kids today are heavier, more given to depression, less creative, and less reflective. How can a Christian mother keep her child from being conformed to the world, but rather, transformed by the renewing of their minds? Family nights, the limiting of extracurricular activity, and homeschooling are all ways Christian families are endeavoring to return to the quiet life. It is also key that we help our children discover things like the joy of reading, crafts, and the outdoors. My research has shown me that the families who are most successful with this have severely limited television watching and computer time. Here is one testimony:

> *Both my parents grew up in homes where the television was the center of family life. It was on during dinner, it provided the background noise throughout the day. When my folks got married, they decided they wanted to raise their children in a TV–free home ... In my parents' opinion, the primary problem with TV isn't the bad things that are watched, it's the good things you're not doing because you're watching—the books that go unread and the stories that go untold. I'm thankful my parents chose books and conversations over television.*[21]

19. If you are a mother, how might you help your children live quieter lives so that they can become reflective adults, like Mary of Bethany?

Review Your Memory Work.

DAY 4

He Is in Control and He Cares

Luke introduces us to Mary of Bethany, but it is John who completes the story. Today and tomorrow we will move into John's gospel to see the rest of the story.

Read John 11:1–44 carefully.

20. Read John 11:1–6 again:

    A. What additional facts do you learn about Mary in this passage?

    B. How does Jesus respond, in verse 4, to the message the sisters send? How would you have interpreted His response if you were one of these women?

    C. What does verse 5 say?

    D. Does verse 6 seem like a contradiction to verse 5 to you? Explain your thinking.

    E. Put yourself in the place of Mary and Martha when their brother dies. What might have been their thoughts and feelings?

    F. Describe a time when you were disappointed by the Lord saying no.

21. Read again John 11:17–27.

    A. Who was the first out when Jesus arrived and what did she say?

    B. How did Jesus respond and what did she think He meant?

    C. What question does Jesus then ask Martha and how does she respond?

Often we give Martha a bad rap, remembering her only as the complaining woman in the kitchen. She was a woman of faith. Not only did she profess faith—great faith in Jesus—she did so right after He allowed her brother to die. She was tried by fire and her core was gold.

22. Read John 11:32-37 again.

    A. Describe the interaction between Mary and Jesus.

    B. Why do you think Jesus wept?

Some say His spirit raged at the last enemy, death. I understand, for I weep at my husband's tomb. Some say He wept because Mary wept, and He loved her. He knew she couldn't see the whole picture, and because she hurt, He hurt. It comforts me so to know He cares and that, though we cannot see the whole picture, He is in control.

23. Is there an application you could make from the above passage to your life?

DAY 5

God Reveals Mysteries to Those Who Hunger and Thirst

Scripture makes it clear that those who hunger and thirst for God are given *more* light. Mary of Bethany understood what all of the other disciples missed.

24. Read Luke 18:31–34 and describe the disciples' understanding of the prophecy which Jesus gave.

25. Read John 12:1–11.

A. Describe what happens in this passage.

Many confuse this incident when Mary of Bethany anointed Jesus for His burial with the incident recorded in Luke 7:36–50. Both of these incidents occurred in the home of Simon. However, in Luke, early in Jesus' ministry, a woman with a sinful past comes to the home of Simon the Pharisee. (Luke's emphasis is that salvation is available to all.) Here, in John, the incident is a different one. Mary of Bethany comes to the home of Simon the Leper (a leper could never be a Pharisee) late in Jesus' ministry, to anoint Jesus for His burial. (John's emphasis is that Jesus is the Christ.)

B. In verses 3 through 6, contrast the illumined heart of Mary with the darkened heart of Judas.

C. Jesus defends Mary, as He did in Luke 10:42. What does He say about her in John 12:7–8?

Speaker Diane Strack tells of visiting an art museum and seeing a painting of Jesus on the cross. Below that painting was another painting of Mary of Bethany anointing Christ with perfume. Mrs. Strack commented that Mary's act helped Jesus to find the strength to go to the cross. The fragrance lingered on Him during the beatings, the carrying of the cross, and the crucifixion.

    D. Scripture tells us that the Lord confides secrets in those who are intimate with Him. How does Mary of Bethany exemplify that?

26. What have you learned from the model of Mary of Bethany? (Be specific.) How could you apply this to your life?

Prayer Time

Lift up your answer to question 26 in prayer and let the other women support you with sentence prayers. When there is a silence, another woman should lift up her request.

Close with a familiar chorus such as "O How He Loves You and Me."

Seventh Stop!
Praying Effectively

Our sons were out of the nest and it wouldn't be long before our daughters took flight as well. I thought my husband and I were entering a new phase of life when he surprised me:

Steve: I think we should adopt again. (We had adopted our youngest daughter, Annie, from Korea.)

I laughed.

Steve: We're finally getting good at parenting—why should we stop now?

I was speechless.

Steve: The overseas orphanages are teeming with children. Let's call Holt International Children's Services and tell them that we're ready for a challenge: an older child, a handicapped child, or a sibling group.

Me: I don't think so.

Steve: Would you be willing to pray about it?

Me: (with great hesitancy) OK.

Steve: Great! Let's go into the living room right now and kneel before God. Let's try to get rid of our own desires and seek His desire.

And so began my refining journey into the heart of God. I will tell you about our journey in this lesson as we examine the Savior's wisdom, as relayed by Luke, on praying effectively.

Prepare Your Heart to Hear

Each day, choose to sit at Jesus' feet, asking Him to help you hear "your portion" for the day. For those reading through all of Luke, do the extra credit each day.

WARMUP

What is one of the nicest gifts you have ever given to someone? Why did you do it?

DAY 1
....

The Basic Principle

Though we are not doing an overview this week, it is still important that you continue to read through Luke. Today read Luke 13—14.

When my husband challenged me to seek God's will concerning a child, I was fearful. What if God's desire was different from mine? I had given my life to the Lord. Yet now I had to consider the state of my heart.

Was I the Lord's servant? Or had I begun arrogantly treating the Lord as if He were my servant?

1. Read and think about Luke 18:9–14.

2. What "reversal" principle does Jesus teach in Luke 18:14?

3. What additional insight or illustrations for the above "reversal" principle are given in:

    A.   Luke 1:52–53

    B.   Luke 6:21

    C.   Luke 6:25

    D.   Luke 10:15

This principle is key to understanding how to live the Christian life. Believers understand that they cannot save themselves, but often they think they can live the Christian life in their own strength. We cannot. Apart from God we can do nothing. We should not be wise in our own eyes, we should not choose our own agenda, and we should not think that we have the power, on our own, to resist temptation, to teach, or to do anything. We must continually, throughout the day, cry out for the mercy of God. An anonymous Russian book of the nineteenth century, *The Way of a Pilgrim,* tells how Christians formed the habit of saying the "Jesus Prayer": *Lord Jesus Christ, have mercy on me.* Inspired by this parable, they tried to learn to say this prayer constantly in the back of their minds, no matter what they were doing. To remind themselves some wore a piece of knotted yarn around a wrist.[22]

Use the following chart to compare the Pharisee and the tax collector.

I. Contrast:	The Pharisee	The Tax Collector
Attitude		
Motive		
Subject		
(God or self)		
Effectiveness before God		

Personal Action Assignment

Tie a string around your wrist to remind you to pray, throughout the day, "Lord Jesus Christ, have mercy on me." Every time you need wisdom, every time you need power, every time you need peace—you need mercy! Tomorrow, record in this space how saying this impacted your attitude and why.

Memory Work

Begin learning the memory passage: Luke 18:13-14.

> *But the tax collector stood at a distance. He would not even look up to heaven, but beat his breast and said, "God, have mercy on me, a sinner."*
>
> *I tell you that this man, rather than the other, went home justified before God. For everyone who exalts himself will be humbled, and he who humbles himself will be exalted.*

DAY 2
. . . .

Ask, Seek, and Knock

When my husband and I knelt before the Lord, I didn't hear anything. No Scripture verses came to mind. No strong impression came to my heart.

Silence.

After what seemed like a long time I looked up. My husband had a stunned look. I said, "What is it?"

He said: "Maybe I imagined it."

"What?"

"While we were praying, I saw a young girl crying."

I was quiet. My husband was not given to hearing voices or seeing visions.

"I don't know, honey," I said. "Maybe because you really want this, you did imagine it."

Steve stood and said, "We'll just keep asking God. We won't rush. We'll wait on Him. He's certainly capable of confirming it if this is His plan."

My husband was so wise. We kept praying, kept knocking, kept seeking.

4. Read Luke 11:5–10

    A. Tell the story of this "nervy" friend.

    B. What does Jesus say, in verse 9, is the point of this story?

    C. Some say you should not bother God with trivial matters (He's too busy!) or that you should not ask more than once (He'll be irritated!) How does this story go against that advice?

The petitioner possesses a focused intensity, as the disciples should have in prayer. The disciple goes to great lengths to make petitions known to God. Thus, the example emerges from a willingness to go next door and ask the friend for help at midnight. There was a "shamelessness" to the asking that reflects how the disciple should pray. Here, Jesus exhorts the believer to pursue an engaging relationship with God and not be deterred by God's greatness.[23]

Darrell Bock

I had often applied the "seek, ask, and knock" passage to continually asking for something I wanted. But more importantly, we must apply this principle to seeking the things that we *know* God wants for us: His wisdom, His strength, His character in us, and His desires for us to be in our hearts. That is what my godly husband was seeking. Some of the Scriptures that seemed to be impressed on Steve's heart at that time were:

Religion that God our Father accepts as pure and faultless is this: to look after orphans and widows in their distress and to keep oneself from being polluted by the world.
James 1:27

If anyone has material possessions and sees his brother in need but has no pity on him, how can the love of God be in him?
1 John 3:17

God's Word is the most reliable way to know God's will. Too often believers seek through circumstances instead of God's Word. Yet when circumstances line up with God's Word, it may be another confirmation.

Later that week, the phone rang. When I heard Barbara Kim's voice I began to feel like the canoe I was in had turned the bend and was now rushing toward the rapids. Barbara worked with Holt International Services. We had adopted our daughter Anne from Korea with Barbara's help—but we had not talked to Barbara in three years. She was excited, having just returned from a trip to an orphanage in Bangkok, Thailand. This was our conversation as I remember it:

Barbara: Dee, we have chosen 12 children out of 500 from that orphanage—children who have spirits of survival. There was one little girl who stole our hearts—and several of us thought of your family.

Me: Why?

Barbara: She reminded us of your oldest daughter. Like Sally, Beth is winsome—with a wonderful smile. All that's wrong with her is that she's missing an arm. It was amputated and she was abandoned as a baby. She's almost 10. Could we send you her picture? Would you be willing to pray?

Me: (with hesitancy) OK. Send the picture. We will pray.

When the envelope arrived I propped it up on the dinner table and waited for Steve to come home. I prayed. I paced. Finally Steve came home and opened the envelope with trembling hands. When a picture of a beautiful young girl fell out, Steve stared at her face. "Yes. This is the little girl whose face I saw."

My heart froze. Didn't God know that I had a full plate? Didn't He care about me and my life?

Again, I had to examine my attitude. Was I willing to lay down my agenda for His? Did I trust that God loved me and knew what was best?

5. Read Luke 11:11–13

    A. What comparison does Jesus make in this passage? Find all you can.

    B. What do you learn about the character of God from this passage?

    C. Why should we be unafraid of God's will?

    D. Is there an application for you in your life?

Continue working on your memory passage.

Close your personal quiet time with "Change My Heart, O God."

DAY 3

Lord, Teach Us to Pray

Concerning the "Lord's Prayer," Dr. Darrell Bock says:

> *Perhaps the most ignored feature of the prayer is that it is a community prayer, not an individual one. Provision, forgiveness, and protection are asked for the community. The lesson of the Lord's Prayer is that we pray not just for the individual, but also for the community, for the spiritual benefit of all who know God.*[24]

We are to be praying for our brothers and sisters in Christ, and this prayer shows us how!

In my quest for peace in adopting Beth, the community of believers played a large part. In particular, three sisters in Christ prayed for me and for our whole family. Each woman sought God's face. It is interesting to me to reflect back and to see how their attitudes in approaching the Lord reflected the principles Jesus taught in Luke 11:2–3.

For example, my soul mate Shell refused to give me advice off the top of her head. Instead, she asked for the morning to seek the Lord. She knew that God was holy ("hallowed be Your name") and so she took her responsibility of counseling me very seriously. She also understood the second principle of the Lord's Prayer ("Thy kingdom come"). When we come to God, it should not be to give Him orders, but to ask Him how we can fit in with His plans for making this world more like His kingdom. Shell asked, "How can the Brestins best fit into Your plan, Lord?"

74

The blueprints for bringing the kingdom to earth are in His Word, so Shell prayerfully searched the Scriptures. Finally, Shell wrote me a ten-page letter filled with Scripture. (I never realized how many Scriptures there were concerning caring for the fatherless and submitting to your husband!)

6. In Luke 11:1–4 find and put in your own words:

   A. The address

   B. The two statements

   C. The three petitions

7. Against what wrong attitudes does Ecclesiastes 5:1–2 warn? What right attitudes does Luke 11:2 teach?

How did Dee's friend Shell exemplify the right attitude?

My next friend, Sara, also helped me to understand the sinfulness in my own heart and how it was impacting me. Jeremiah tells us we have deceitful hearts. This is one of the reasons we need each other in the community of believers—to help us to see our blind spots! Solomon says the purposes of our hearts are like dark waters—but a friend of understanding can draw those waters out (Prov. 20:5). After prayer, Sara probed to try to understand why I was reluctant. This was our conversation:

Sara: Are you afraid because of her age? Do you think that because she is almost 10 it's too late to mold her?

Me: No. I can't imagine taking a baby or a toddler. I'm too tired! I'm glad she's almost 10.

Sara: Are you afraid because she is missing an arm that you will forever be helping her?

Me: No. Steve tells me that those who've been without a limb for a long time have learned how to do practically everything for themselves.

Then I began to share with Sara that my husband, who was an orthopedic surgeon, had said Beth would do some things with her feet and her teeth. I began to cry, admitting to Sara that it would embarrass me. At that moment we both realized that at least part of my hesitancy was due to an unmerciful attitude.

Again and again, Luke shows us that Jesus is longing for those who say they belong to God to live lives of purity and mercy. He is angry at the Pharisees for their hypocrisy. He weeps over Jerusalem. He pleads with His listeners to live lives that reflect God's kingdom! As my friends prayed for me, God revealed the impurity and hardness of my heart.

How we need to continually be praying for one another in the body of Christ, not in a rote way, with meaningless memorized phrases, but with passion that God's holiness and mercy will grow in our collective hearts!

O God, You are our FATHER! May we live like Your children!

O God, You are HOLY! May we be holy!

O God, bring Your heavenly KINGDOM to earth. Use us as Your vessels to do so!

And then, Father, please:

PROVIDE for us.

PARDON us and empower us to truly pardon others.

PROTECT us from the wiles of the evil one.

8. Matthew's version of what is often called The Lord's Prayer is more familiar and, many feel, more lyrical than the abbreviated version Luke give us. The fact that these versions are slightly different confirms that what was being taught here is not so much a particular set of "magic words," but important principles. It certainly can be prayed individually, but it is a corporate prayer, so think of it as well in terms of the body of believers. Notice how much of the prayer is dedicated to shaping our trust and character. In each of the phrases, state the principle. Then, pray it, making it personal. Some of the answers are provided; some need to be filled in.

   A. *Father, hallowed be your name*

      (1) Principle:

Recognizing that God is both personal (Father) and holy (hallowed)

      (2) My prayer:

Thank You for being our Father. May we not forget how holy You are.

   B. *your kingdom come*

      (1) Principle:

Ask God to bring His kingdom, to right wrongs, to show His full justice and authority. Ask Him to help us be His vessels to do so.

      (2) My prayer:

   C. *Give us each day our daily bread.*

      (1) Principle:

      (2) My prayer:

D. *Forgive us our sins, for we forgive everyone who sins against us*

   (1) Principle:

   (2) My prayer:

E. *And lead us not into temptation*

   (1) Principle:

If temptation is to be avoided, God must lead the way.

   (2) My prayer:

DAY 4

Change My Heart, O God

Elisa Morgan, President of M.O.P.S. International (Mothers-of-Preschoolers), dramatized our arrogance in approaching God as if He is a vending machine. "We put in our three minutes of prayer, we wait three minutes, and then we say, 'Where are the goods?'" (Wildly, she started kicking the machine.)

How often we are like that. Most prayer requests are for those with illness, financial needs, or some sort of trouble. While that is perfectly legitimate, how we fail to pray for our hearts, for our character, as the Lord keeps teaching us to do. My greatest prayer need in the crisis I faced in deciding to adopt Beth was my heart. When my husband was dying of cancer, I pleaded for healing on earth, but my husband, though he *did* ask for healing on earth (and one day we will understand why it was refused), more often asked for the character and the strength to glorify God in his suffering—to be faithful to the end. And God granted him a heart, despite 14 months of enormous suffering, that glorified God to his dying breath.

It is easy to look at the religious leaders of Jesus' day and be very critical, but if we are honest, often we can be like them. They did not guard their hearts, and so often, our hearts are not our primary concern. How wonderful it would be if we would ask our friends to pray for pure and loving hearts.

9. Read Luke 11:33–36 remembering that light is a metaphor for God's Word. In verse 33, what does a man do with a light and why?

10. A. What is Jesus telling us?

B. To understand the metaphor in 34–36, a good eye is one that is filled with good light. What warning is given in verse 35?

C. What does this mean? How can we "see to it" that the light within us is not darkness?

We are so naturally depraved that we tend to pray selfishly. This is one of the reasons why godly saints have learned to pray through Scripture. The Word of God is light, and it purifies our praying. Many great believers have had the habit, no matter what else they are studying, of regularly praying through the Psalms.

11. We certainly do not want to be like the Pharisees. To help avoid this, to help keep the light within us pure, we need to look carefully at the criticisms Jesus had of them and to make sure they are *not* true of us. In each of the following, find the criticism/exhortation and then, consider how to apply it personally.

A. Luke 11:37–41

Criticism/exhortation:

Application:

B. Luke 11:42

Criticism/exhortation

Application:

C. Luke 11:43–46

Criticism/exhortation

Application:

As I began to pray about my heart, and as I immersed myself in the pure light of God's Word, He truly did change my heart. His grace also began to flow. Part of that grace was my friend Janet who told me that if we adopted Beth, she would love to help me. She said that Beth could come to her home daily to learn English. By now I had not only a peace, but an excitement.

Review your memory work.

DAY 5

Don't Give Up!

That didn't mean that our adoption journey was easy! There were plenty of times when we came boldly to the Lord asking Him to tame a new lion that had sprung out in our path!

One lion was my schedule. I was booked to be the keynote speaker at women's conferences three out of four weekends. We were told that on short notice we would need to fly to Thailand and stay there for two weeks. Anxious thoughts filled my heart: How could I break my word to these conferences at the last minute? And yet, if I didn't, how would our new daughter (and the Thai adoption officials!) feel if Steve came alone?

I am hesitant to dictate specific requests to God, for who am I to tell the One who made the universe what to do? And yet, He was my Father and I needed help! Alan Redpath has pointed out that prayer should be more than just asking God to bless some folks and keep us plugging along; prayer is warfare! [26]

As I looked through my calendar I found a two-week free period beginning February 14th, and so, I said, "Lord, unless You have a better idea, could we please be asked to fly to Thailand on February 14th?"

On January 20th, we got the phone call from Holt.

Barbara: "Pack your bags, Dee! It's time for you and Steve to go get your daughter!"

I held my breath. "When?"

Barbara: "February 1st!"

My heart dropped. I had been bold, but God seemed to be saying no. I knew I couldn't go to Thailand—I had committed to three retreats in the first two weeks of February. The authorities in Thailand agreed our daughter Sally could go in my place and, with a heavy heart, I bought airplane tickets for my husband and daughter.

Frankly, it didn't even occur to me to *keep* on praying for February 14th—I thought that door was shut! But the women who were coordinating a retreat I was giving in Wichita in early February felt badly that I had to be with them instead of in Thailand. So *they* persisted in prayer and encouraged me to persist. We prayed the authorities in Thailand would change their minds and postpone the date for two weeks!

A few days before Steve and Sally were to leave, Barbara called and asked: "Dee, is there any chance you could go on February 14th? Thailand has postponed your date by two weeks!"

I changed the dates of the tickets (we had not originally planned to take Sally—but she proved crucial in helping Beth feel at ease) and I bought a third ticket for me. I have thanked God so many times for allowing me to go.

I will never forget Beth's radiant face when we met her. This was a child who, at the time Steve and I prayed, had given up hope of ever having a home and was despairing. It overwhelms me to realize God heard her cry. A little girl who is not valued in our world is of great value to God. In part, this is the message of Luke.

Beth has become a beautiful young woman who knows the Lord. However, I hope if our story had not had a happy ending I would still trust the Lord and keep on persisting in prayer for Beth.

Let us close with one last story, another woman's story, another unique to Luke. It is the story of the persistent widow and the unjust judge. It teaches us persistence in prayer, but it also teaches us not to give up in a bigger picture. This world is full of sorrow and suffering, and there are going to be times when we will long for the return of Jesus, for vindication, for His Kingdom to come on earth.

12. Read through Luke 17:20–37 for a context of the story of the persistent widow. What is the subject of this passage? (This is a difficult passage, and a fascinating one, but since this is just a 12-week study, I am only asking for you to identify the subject of this passage.)

13. Read Luke 18:1–8 and find your answers in the passage.

   A. Describe the judge. Find whatever you can.

   B. What key word would you use to describe the widow?

   C. Why does the judge give in?

   D. How is God different than the judge?

14. Remembering that this parable follows warnings concerning suffering in the end times, what is the message to the disciples of Jesus and to us?

If you need to suffer at the end of your life, whether it is through disease or persecution in the end times, what will you remember from this parable?

Not only should we not give up "at the end of our earthly lives," we should not give up in pleading with God for help every day of our lives. Every moment we are in need of His mercy. This parable is followed by the story we studied in day one, of the publican crying out for mercy. Can you say your memory passage?

15. Summarize the main lessons you have learned about prayer.

Prayer Time

On an index card, write down a bold request for your character, for your heart, or for deliverance from a sin that plagues you. You can sign your name or keep it anonymous. Place the cards in the middle of the table, mix, and take one. Pray for this person persistently in the next week.

Eighth Stop!
Fear God and Nothing Else

Another subject Luke frequently addresses is possessions. Luke, and Luke alone, has three different stories about "a certain rich man." There is the rich fool, the rich man with an unjust steward, and the rich man and Lazarus. Each parable, though having its own emphasis, shows that if we truly fear God it will affect dramatically how we handle our possessions. Interspersed between these parables are reassurances that if we fear God, we do not need to fear anything or anyone else. If we seek God, we do not need to seek anything or anyone else. This is the radical wisdom of Christ concerning possessions—and it permeates the gospel of Luke.

Quite honestly, I don't know too many believers who truly live according to the radical wisdom of Christ in this area. Those who do, stand out. My friend Ellen is a single missionary who has joyfully seen God provide for her as she moves from one mission field to another. When she is called to move on, she doesn't cling to the meager possessions she has, but gives them away! Then she writes, with almost a holy hilarity, telling her friends of how God provided in the next place!

Our friends the Wiebes are the reason Steve and I were drawn to live in Kearney, Nebraska 25 years ago. Steve wanted to be in partnership with David Wiebe. Here was a "rich man," a doctor, who didn't trust in his riches, but in God. Therefore, the bottom line was not money, but patient care. If a patient couldn't pay, it didn't matter. If a partner wanted to spend time on the mission field and wouldn't be drawing an income for a while, that was wonderful! If the doctors couldn't see as many patients because they were giving them very good care, and therefore putting less money in the "pot," that was as it should be! If God blessed them financially, they had more to give away! Though David and his wife Lorma are definitely storing up treasures in heaven, they don't live like ascetics, but truly enjoy and appreciate the aesthetic value of beautiful wood, windows, and wares from around the world, seeing them as the good things God gives us to enjoy. David frequently ministers at a hospital in India, and their home is filled with the lavish paintings that David himself and their daughter have painted of these beautiful people. Lorma also opened a Mennonite shop in our town, "Ten Thousand Villages," which takes the beautiful handmade wares of third world craftsmen, sells them to "rich Americans," and then sends the money back to the craftsmen.

The truths that Luke teaches about possessions are repeated at the close of 1 Timothy when Paul charges those who are rich in this present age (and truly, that is all Americans) not "to trust in uncertain riches but in the living God, who gives us all things richly to enjoy" and to be "rich in good works, ready to give, willing to share," so that they may store up for themselves "a good foundation for the time to come."

Prepare Your Heart to Hear

Each day, choose to sit at Jesus' feet, asking Him to help you hear "your portion" for the day. For those reading through all of Luke, do the extra credit each day.

Memory Review

Review Luke 1:46–50; 9:23–25; 10:41–42; and Luke 18:13–14 this week. Prepare to say these verses in twos when you meet for discussion.

WARMUP

Share a time, in a sentence, when you know God provided materially for you.

DAY 1

Overview

Read Luke 15—16.

1. What stood out to you from this week's introduction?

2. Look at 1 Timothy 6:17–19 and find all the instructions you can to "rich men." (You will see them again in Luke this week.)

3. Read Luke 12:4–7 and write down whom we should not fear, and why, and whom we should fear, and why.

4. Review Luke 1:46–50 today. What parallel truth do you see in this passage and in Luke 12:4–7?

DAY 2

Take Heed and Beware of Covetousness

Luke often sets up a parable with an incident that explains why Jesus addresses the topic. In this case, two brothers are arguing about the division of their inheritance. It is possible the one brother is keeping it all, and so the other brother appeals to Jesus, asking Him to speak to his brother.

Most of us will face this kind of scenario, because in the western world we are rich, and parents tend to have goods to leave to their children. Many siblings stop speaking to each other after trying to divide the goods.

Read Luke 12:13–15

5. Rabbis were often called upon to handle disputes. What was the request that a man made of Jesus in Luke 12:13?

6. What question does Jesus ask the man?

> *The reply apparently urges the man to settle his own affairs. But with it comes a warning that something more destructive may be going on. Jesus feared that the issue of possessions would become a barrier between the man and his brother.*
> Darrell Bock [27]

7. Both Martha and this brother came to Jesus with a complaint about their sibling. What similarities do you see between His response in Luke 10:41–42 and Luke 12:14–15? What differences? How do you imagine each sibling may have felt about the rebuke?

8. What is the warning Jesus gives the brother and the disciples in verse 15?

9. Imagine some situations you might face, if you have siblings, and if you may need to divide goods. How will you respond? Or, if it has already happened, do you feel you responded as Jesus would have had you respond?

10. How might you specifically apply the warning of Jesus in Luke 12:15 to your life? Be still before God and ask Him to show you specifics. What are they?

Review your memory work of Luke 9:23–24.

DAY 3

The Rich Fool

We certainly don't want to be what Scripture describes as a fool. Though this person may pretend to be religious, in his heart, he says there is no God (Ps. 14:1). He thinks he is always right (Prov. 12:15), uses anger to control (Prov. 14:16), and trusts in his own heart (Prov. 28:26). A fool's life is all about himself, and he does not care for the needs of others. Jesus himself says it a serious thing to call someone a fool without cause (Matt. 5:22). Yet there truly *are* fools out there, and Scripture warns us to stay away from them and to have teachable hearts so we do not become like them. Jesus follows his warning to "take heed and beware of covetousness" with an illustration about "a rich fool." He who has ears, let him hear!

11. Read Luke 12:16–21.

    A. Describe what happens in this story.

    B. How many times does the fool use the word "I"? Significance?

    C. A parable always has one central point. Jesus states it at the close. What is it?

    D. How does this parable illustrate the warning Jesus gave to the brother in Luke 12:15?

    E. How might you apply the central point: "So is he who lays up treasure for himself, and is not rich toward God" (v. 21, NKJV).

12. What is the primary teaching in Luke 12:22–34?

13. Why do you think the above teaching follows the parable of the rich fool?

Luke gives us another parable that further helps us understand what it means to be "rich toward God." We'll look at that tomorrow.

Review your memory work of Luke 10:40–42.

DAY 4

The Parable of the Prudent Steward

The most stirring sermon I have ever heard on giving came from a preacher who was 95. He sat on a stool, his white head a "crown of glory," and his face radiant.

When he and his wife were in their twenties, they prayerfully planned their "eternal investments," choosing missionaries that they felt had passion, talent, and wisdom. 70 years later he told of the thrill they had in seeing their "seed" reap such bountiful harvest, "…far and above," he said, "our wildest hopes. A packet of seeds became a field of waving grain!" One couple, with their financial help, had started a tiny hospital in Africa. That hospital had quadrupled in size and staff and had ministered over the last 70 years to hundreds of thousands of Africans both physically and spiritually. Another woman had translated the Bible into an Indian dialect and had seen many villagers embrace the Word in their own language, come to a saving knowledge of Christ, and were multiplying down through the generations. He shared also that God had always provided for him and his wife, above and beyond what they truly needed.

On and on this wise old man shared, glowing, urging us to be shrewd in our eternal investments, to be rich toward God, and to never worry that God would fail to take care of us!

The following parable has been confusing to many. Why would Jesus give us a model of a "dishonest manager" to emulate? Darrell Bock says that though the man was an unrighteous man, the correct interpretation may be that "when he was told he would be let go, he reacted wisely but still honestly by removing his commission."[28]

14. Read Luke 16:1–9.

   A. Describe the dilemma of the employee who had wasted his employer's possessions. When the manager suspected he would be fired, what was his reasonable fear? (Luke 16:1–4).

   B. It is not illegal to get a commission on goods sold, and here, the manager is able to remove it from the debtors. Describe what he does (Luke 16:5–7).

C. How does his employer respond to his manager's plan? (Luke 16:8). How did this action benefit his employer? How did it benefit himself?

D. What is the point of the parable? (v. 9)

God's children should be more intentional about how they pursue life. In particular, they should use "unrighteous mammon" (that is, possessions, not just money) in a way that makes friends...This sort of kindness will allow "them" to receive those who practice it into eternal habitations. The "them" alludes to the angels, as a picture of heaven's acceptance. Darrell Bock [29]

15. What application could you make from the above parable?

16. What principles concerning possessions does Jesus give in:
    A. Luke 16:10–11

    B. Luke 16:13

    C. Luke 16:15

17. Do you sense that you should be diligent to make an application to any of the above principles? If so, what?

18. Read the story of the rich man and Lazarus in Luke 16:19–31.
    A. Summarize what happened.

    B. What is the central point of this parable?

    C. How was the statement of Luke 16:31 fulfilled?

Review your memory work of Luke 18:13–14.

DAY 5
....

The Rich Young Ruler

This story is told in all of the Synoptic Gospels. Undoubtedly it made an impression on the disciples. So often we admire those who are rich, or beautiful, or famous in this life. But there will be a great reversal one day if they don't know the Lord. They may appear to be religious, but God can see their heart, and He knows if He is loved by them or not.

19. Read Luke 18:18–23.

    A. Describe what happens in this incident.

    B. Find three things that reveal the man's insincerity.

Jesus could see the man's heart. Jesus challenges his flattery, challenges his self-righteous claim, and finally, reveals his heart when he asks what the man will not do.

20. Deuteronomy 30:15–20 has a similar teaching to the above story. What choice is given to the Israelites, with what consequence for each choice?

21. Read Luke 18:24–30.
    A. What does Jesus say, when the rich young ruler chooses his riches over God?

    B. What is the reaction of the disciples?

It is almost as if they are thinking: *If the rich and powerful may not be saved, what hope do they have?*

    C. What reassurance does Jesus give in verse 27?

    D. What good news does Jesus give in verses 29–30? What other parable in this lesson teaches the same truth?

22. Read Luke 19:1–10
    A. What happens in this incident?

    B. Why might the disciples have been surprised to hear Jesus say that salvation has come to the home of Zacchaeus?

    C. Contrast Zacchaeus with the rich young ruler. Find everything you can.

Jesus didn't ask Zacchaeus to give everything because he had a truly repentant heart. Here is a rich man entering heaven!

23. Summarize what you have learned from Luke about possessions. Share at least three points that you want to remember.

Prayer Time

Instead of sharing individual prayer requests, have each woman lift her own request up in prayer. Then have a few women support her with sentences. When there is a silence, another woman should lift up her individual prayer request. Close with a familiar chorus such as "Shout to the Lord."

Ninth Stop!
Parables That Women Love

How we love the parable of the prodigal son! Prodigals all, we bathe in the warmth and comfort of the Father's love:

But when he was yet a great way off, his father saw him, and had compassion, and ran, and fell on his neck, and kissed him (Luke 15:20 KJV).

This poignant scene is the third in a trio of paintings. Only Luke portrays the stories of the lost sheep, the lost coin, and the lost son. These pictures touch our hearts because, as Barbara Brown Taylor, then rector of Grace-Calvary Church, writes:

> *I am the poor, tuckered-out lamb, draped across my dear redeemer's shoulders so full of gratitude and relief that I vow never to wander away from him again. Or I am the silver coin, lying in some dark corner of the universe until the good woman who will not give up on me sweeps me into the light.* [30]

Yet as comforting as it is to identify with the found in each of these illustrations, God wants us to go deeper. First, He wants us to identify with the seeker—with the shepherd who is rejoicing over his recovered lamb and with the housewife who is jumping up and down because she has found her lost coin!

Prepare Your Heart to Hear

Before each of the following five devotional times, quiet your heart and ask God to speak to you personally from His Word.

WARMUP

Share a time when you lost something important (pet, ring, car, child ...) and then found it! How did you feel before and after?

Memory Work:

But when he was yet a great way off, his father saw him, and had compassion, and ran, and fell on his neck, and kissed him.   Luke 15:20 KJV

DAY 1

Overview

Continue to read in Luke 17—18.

Read Luke 15:1–2.

1. Describe the context of this three-pictured parable. What were the religious leaders missing?

Read Luke 15:3–32.

While we think of these as three parables, accurately, it is one parable with three illustrations. (Jesus told them "this parable.") Therefore, the central point is the same in each.

2. In each of these pictures, find evidence for the seekers:

3. In each of these illustrations, the seeker responds similarly upon finding the lost. Describe the response.

What is Jesus trying to help us to understand?

	Sheep	Coin	Son
Anguish			
Joy			

DAY 2

Developing Our Father's Eyes

Chuck Swindoll asks: "Remember when you first became a Christian? You would lie on your bed thinking 'Who can I tell?' That's exactly how it was for me. I was highly motivated to share my faith because I had compassion for individuals who were wandering in the darkness from which I had been so recently delivered. But so often, as our eyes have grown accustomed to the light, we forget the misery of being lost."

The most fruitful Christians evangelistically are new Christians. They remember what it is like to be lost. THEY CARE!

In addition to developing compassion, we must ask for wisdom on how to approach the lost. People are lost for different reasons. Some, like the prodigal son, have rebelled. Others, like the poor little sheep, simply don't know the right path. And then there are those who are like the lost coin, who are lost because of the carelessness of others. For years I was part of the reason that one of my family members was slow in coming to Christ. I would argue with her about issues that were not central to salvation, such as abortion or homosexuality. When I asked her forgiveness for being so obnoxious and started showing her the love of the Father, the walls came down. Respected author John Stott says: "We must struggle to listen through their ears and look through their eyes so as to grasp what prevents them from hearing the gospel and seeing Christ."[31]

4. Who are some of the lost in your life? How might you discover what it is that is keeping them from Christ?

Personal Action Assignment

Pray for the lost in your life. Write the names God impresses on your heart in your journal. Ask God to give you compassion and wisdom. Write down any thoughts you receive.

DAY 3

Grace and Ungrace

In Philip Yancey's powerful book *What's So Amazing about Grace?,* he says that in Jesus' day, "the worse a person felt about herself, the more likely she saw Jesus as a refuge."[32] Today, many who are acutely aware of their sin stay away from church because Christians make them feel worse, not better! Yancey believes that is because we are not showing grace but ungrace. We have forgotten how to show grace. We need to study the portrait of the "lovesick father."

And the son said unto him, Father, I have sinned against heaven, and in thy sight, and am no more worthy to be called thy son.

But the father said to his servants, Bring forth the best robe, and put it on him; and put a ring on his hand, and shoes on his feet.
—Luke 15:21–22, KJV

Read Luke 15:11–24.

5. List evidences of the Father's grace. (Give references.)

Read Luke 15:25–32.

6. List evidences of the Father's grace toward the older brother.

7. How have believers shown grace to you? Can you recall a specific time? How did it impact you?

Jim Wallis, editor of Sojourners, *says: "Evangelical Christians are big on salvation but often short on grace."[33] Grace is a most unnatural act, Philip Yancey says. We are reluctant to give grace because it is so costly. (It costs the recipient nothing but it costs the giver a great deal!) However, as costly as grace is, ungrace costs more. We imprison ourselves in a jail of icy bitterness, cutting ourselves off from those who are dearest to us and we pass on a habit of ungrace to our children and grandchildren.*

8. Look up the word "grace." Define it. Then come up with a definition of "ungrace."

9. Remember the questions of who, what, where, how, and why. Take a few of them and see what you can discover in Luke 15:25–32. What new observations do you have?

10. Luke is full of examples of "ungrace": The Pharisees, the townspeople, and even, at times, the disciples. Here are a few examples, ending with the older brother. Imagine what the cost of "ungrace" might have been to those they hurt and to the perpetrators themselves.

   A. Luke 6:1–11

   B. Luke 7:44–47

   C. Luke 9:51–56

   D. Luke 10:30–37

   E. Luke 15:25–32

11. As you are still before the Lord, how might you be more gracious toward the people in your life?

DAY 4

Prodigals All

Prodigal means "wasteful" and there is some of the prodigal in all of us. We have rebelled against the discipline of the Father, wanting to be free and to do what we want to do with our money, time, and talent. German author Helmut Thielicke, in *The Waiting Father*, comments how rare the quiet and peaceful home is today, even among Christians, because we are not really abiding in Christ.

> *Is not Europe, is not the Christian Western world on this same road of separation from its origin and the source of its blessings?*

> *Each age has its own peculiar "far country," and so has ours...It is true that we work with the Father's capital, with our energy and ambition, our highly developed reason, our technical skills...all these things which the Father has given us! But we use them without him....That's why what we possess explodes in our hands....That's why modern man has bad dreams as soon as he is alone and has a little time for reflection. That's why he has to turn on the radio or run to the movies to divert himself....He cannot be alone; he must have diversion....But when he cannot and therefore must, then he is no longer free!*

> *The repentance of the lost son is therefore not something merely negative.... Whenever the New Testament speaks of repentance, always the great joy is in the background. It does not say, "Repent or hell will swallow you up," but "Repent, the kingdom of heaven is at hand."* [34]

Ask yourself if Helmut Thielicke's reflections apply to you. Are there areas where you are rebelling against the discipline of the Lord? Are you seeking to divert yourself to anesthetize the pain? Come home and experience the joy!

12. We are less likely to wander away if we appreciate what we have at home.

    A. Recall the darkness! Share three ways Jesus has changed your life. If you came to Christ as a child, share three ways your life might be different had you never come to the Light.

    B. Think about the times when you have been particularly close to Jesus. Recall the joy and the peace.

    C. List some of the blessings in your life right now.

13. Review the memory passages. As you do:
    A. Describe the joy Mary had in being close to the Father in Luke 1:46-50.

    B. Describe the discipline of God and how it leads to blessing in Luke 9:23-25..

C. Describe the blessing Mary of Bethany receives by staying close to God in Luke 10:41-42.

D. Describe the love of the Father in Luke 15:20.

DAY 5

* *

When Someone You Love Is a Prodigal

My husband returned to our bedroom at 2 a.m. after checking on our fifteen-year-old son. Steve sat on the edge of the bed, his head between his hands.

"What is it?" I asked.

"John's gone. His bed is empty. His window is open."

We imagined, correctly, that he was out with his new friends, older boys who liked to party, boys John had met at his new job. My husband and I held each other and prayed for John.

The next six months were some of the most difficult we had ever experienced as a family. John was rebellious and moody—so different from the obedient and joyful boy we'd known for 15 years. He suffered the consequences of some of his wrong choices, and as painful as it was, we did not try to intervene to spare him those consequences. However, we did give him love and support.

Perhaps the most helpful thing we did during that time was to try to maintain our relationship. My godly friend Shirley Ellis advised me: "Even though you are angry with John, show him you love him. If you can't talk to him, give him backrubs, play chess with him." My sister Sally fasted and prayed with me that God would protect John during his prodigal journey and bring him safely back to Himself.

One night I received a phone call from our youth pastor asking if a traveling Nebraska football player could stay at our house. When I told John that Travis Turner would be our guest, John's eyes lit up. "Travis Turner? Here? In our house?" Travis was not only well known in Nebraska for football, he loved the Lord and was responsive to His Spirit. Travis stayed up with John until the wee hours of the morning, talking to him about his walk with Christ. The next day John came to us and said, "I've sinned against God and against you. I'm going to quit my job, become active in the youth group, and find new, *godly* friends. And I'm going to memorize the Sermon on the Mount in the next three months so that I can walk the kind of walk Travis Turner walks." And John kept his word. Today, 15 years later, John is still walking with the Lord, a godly husband and father. How I thank God for restoring our son to Himself.

14. As difficult as it is, sometimes we need to allow a child to experience the pain of wrong choices. How do you see this in the parable of the two sons? (Give references.)

What are some ways a mother might allow her child to experience the pain of wrong choices?

15. We need to continue to show our children love, even if they hurt or disappoint us. How do you see this in the father's attitude toward both of his sons? (Give references.)

What are some ways a mother might show her prodigal child love without endorsing his wrong choices?

16. How has God allowed you to experience the pain of wrong choices?

How has He shown you love even when you disappointed Him?

If time permits, give an opportunity for women to share what they think they will remember from this lesson.

Prayer Time

Pair up in twos. Have a time of thanksgiving for ways God has shown grace to you. Confess silently or audibly ways you have rebelled at God's discipline. Then pray for lost loved ones. Close with Psalm 51:10–13.

The Savior's Victory

Some of our women amazed us.
They went to the tomb early this
morning but didn't find his body.
They came and told us that they
had seen a vision of angels,
who said he was alive.
—Luke 24:22–23

The Savior's Victory
(Luke 22—24)

Dark events swirl around the Savior in Luke 22 and 23. Luke makes it clear this is a spiritual battle. C. S. Lewis captured the drama of this spiritual battle in his allegory, *The Lion, the Witch, and the Wardrobe*. Lucy and Susan sense that something dreadful is about to happen and crouch behind the bushes. They watch a spiritual battle between Aslan and the witch's army of ogres, hags, cruels, and ettins. Aslan's great mane is sheared, his jaw muzzled, and he is tied to a stone table.

> *Then the ogre stood back and the children, watching from their hiding place, could see the face of Aslan looking all small and different without its mane. The enemies also saw the difference.*
>
> *"Why, he's only a great cat after all!" cried one.... And they surged round Aslan, jeering at him, saying things like "Puss, Puss! Poor Pussy."*

The children wait for Aslan's roar to spring upon his enemies, but it doesn't happen. Instead, the witch draws near:

> *She stood by Aslan's head. Her face was working and twitching with passion, but he looked up at the sky, still quiet, neither angry nor afraid, but a little sad. Then, just before she gave the blow, she stooped down and said in a quivering voice,*
>
> *"And now, who has won? Fool, did you think that by all this you would save the human traitor? Now I will kill you instead of him as our pact was and so the Deep Magic will be appeased . . ."*
>
> *The children did not see the actual moment of the killing. They couldn't bear to look and had covered their eyes.*

The witch has magic, but Aslan has deeper magic, magic that has existed, Lewis says, from "before the dawn of time." Days later:

> *There, shining in the sunrise, larger than they had seen him before, shaking his mane (for it had apparently grown again) stood Aslan himself.*
>
> *"You're not—not a—?" asked Susan in a shaky voice. She couldn't bring herself to say the word ghost. Aslan stooped his golden head and licked her forehead. The warmth of his breath and a rich sort of smell that seemed to hang about his hair came all over her.*
>
> *"Do I look it?" he said.*
>
> *"Oh, you're real, you're real! Oh, Aslan!" cried Lucy, and both girls flung themselves upon him and covered him with kisses.* [35]

Satan is powerful, and you will see that he put up a tremendous fight here to destroy Jesus. Yet, killing Jesus, says Walter Wink, was like trying to destroy a dandelion seedhead by blowing on it. [36]

Tenth Stop!
The Savior's Farewell

Have you ever moved away from friends and family? Or felt the pain of a child leaving for college, marriage, or the mission field? Some of the most poignant words written are about such parting scenes. Shakespeare said, "Parting is such sweet sorrow." Amy Carmichael writes of "the rending" between her and the man who had become like a father to her when she felt the call to the mission field in China. She felt she would break his heart if she left him, but the call was clear. She stood at the rail of the ship, looking at his dear wrinkled face, perhaps, she thought, for the last time. Fifty-two years later she wrote:

> *Never, I think, not even in Heaven shall I forget that parting. It was such a rending thing that I never wanted to repeat it ... Even now my heart winces at the thought of it. The night I sailed for China, March 3, 1893, my life, on the human side was broken, and it never was mended again.* [37]

This was the intense emotion Jesus was feeling. John tells us Jesus "loved them unto the end" (John 13:1, KJV). Luke tells us He "eagerly" desired to eat this Passover with them (Luke 22:15). Literally, He says, "With desire I have desired," reflecting the intensity. It is as if one were to have a last Christmas Eve with those who were the very dearest on earth to her before she was to die on Christmas Day.

Prepare Your Heart to Hear

Father, help me put myself in the place of those to whom this actually happened. Make it live for me.

Memory Work

In this victory oasis you will memorize Luke 23:28; 24:38–39.

> *Jesus turned and said to them, "Daughters of Jerusalem, do not weep for me; weep for yourselves and for your children."* Luke 23:28

WARMUP

Describe a parting scene you have witnessed or experienced. What were the emotions?

DAY I

Overview

Read Luke 19-20.

Dr. Darrell Bock writes:

> *Sinister forces are behind Jesus' death ... the events surrounding Jesus' ministry are part of a larger, cosmic drama between great spiritual powers. Heaven and hell are interested in the fate of Jesus. In the great chess match, this is Satan's major move to remove Jesus from the game.*[38]

1. Read all of the introductory notes. Comment on what stood out to you from:
   A. The introductory notes for THE FOURTH OASIS: The Savior's Victory (p. 99)

In what ways does C. S. Lewis communicate that the battle was a spiritual battle with dark forces?

   B. The introductory notes for THE TENTH STOP! The Savior's Farewell (p. 100)

Read Luke 22 as an overview.
2. Find evidence for the fact that this is a spiritual battle, but Jesus is in control. (Give verse references.)

Spend five minutes on the memory passage.

Journal Entry: What did God impress on your heart? Make a brief entry in your journal.

DAY 2

Meaningful Meals and Celebrations

For us as Christians, Christmas, Easter, and Thanksgiving are our most important and festive holidays. For the Jews, the most important holiday time was Passover. As with us, this time was set apart for remembering, for showing love to family, and for celebrating with feasting, music, and tradition!

For us as women, holidays are important, because we often are the ones who seize them as an opportunity to show love. Likewise, meals are important to us, because we are often the ones preparing them, longing to make them vessels of love. Intriguingly, holidays, celebrations, and meals are important in Luke, perhaps because one of his primary sources was women.

Here, in Luke 22, Jesus prepares to celebrate the Passover meal with His loved ones. Today we will look at the significance of meals in Luke, and of celebrations, and of seizing them to glorify God and to show love. Tomorrow we will look at why Passover was the time that God chose to have the Savior die.

3. Meals should be a way of showing love, of celebrating God's goodness, or of being a catalyst for intimate conversation. How can you see this in the following passages?

   A. Luke 9:13–17

   B. Luke 14:12–14

   C. Luke 15:22–24

4. Meals, as God intended, should be a time of showing love. But they can be ruined. In a phrase, what was lacking in each of the following scenes?

   A. What did Simon the Pharisee lack? (Luke 7:44–47)

   B. What did Martha lack? (Luke 10:38–42)

   C. What did those invited lack? (Luke 14:15–24)

   D. What did the older brother lack? (Luke 15:25–30)

5. What can a woman do to increase the chances that there will be a spirit of love and graciousness at family meals?

What can a woman do to facilitate meaningful conversation at meals shared with family or friends?

If, on Christmas Day, you suspected that it would be your last, the day would be particularly poignant. Harold Shaw experienced this when he had lung cancer. In *God in the Dark*, Luci Shaw describes some of the emotions that she saw in her husband on that Christmas Day. I think Jesus had similar feelings the night of His last Passover Supper.

> *Christmas Day. Bright, clear, minus three degrees... We opened presents, and I took lots of photographs...*
>
> *After baked ham, we had cake in the family room. It seemed natural to suggest that we all pray for Harold. "But first," he said, "I want to read you some of the Bible passages that have come alive for me in the last few weeks." Harold is a good reader, but he struggled with the words and his emotions as he read. Then he prayed for each of us in the room, for the future mates of John, Jeff, and Kris, and for all our grandchildren, born and yet to be born, blessing us all in the name of Christ.*
>
> *One by one, each of us was crying, out of our grief and incredulity, our sense of loss, pain, and fear. Kris lay sobbing on the couch, her feet in H.'s lap and her head in Marian's lap. It was a good, hard, precious, difficult, close, intense, unifying time...[39]*

6. What would be some of the things you would want to do if you were spending your last Christmas with your loved ones?

Why might it be wise to create an opportunity for your loved ones to express their feelings for each other at the next holiday gathering? How might you facilitate that opportunity?

In our family we often have a time of "blessing" each other by having each person share specific reasons why they are thankful for the person on their right or left. Or, if the gathering is a smaller holiday gathering, we each bless each guest.

Group Action Assignment

Plan a meal together at which you will bless one another!

7. At the meal in Luke 22:24–32, find an instance when:

A. Jesus instructs them.

B. Jesus thanks or blesses them.

C. Jesus warns, encourages, and instructs Simon.

DAY 3

I Have Eagerly Desired to Eat This Passover with You

The Passover meal was the most important of the Jewish feasts, a time when the nation reflected on its deliverance. It was no coincidence that Jesus, our Passover Lamb, died at this time. God planned the year, the day, and the hour. The Passover lambs were sacrificed on the fourteenth day of the month of Nisan between the hours of 2:30 p.m. and 5:30 p.m. That is precisely the time when Jesus, our perfect Lamb of God, died.

And Jesus knew He would not be there to eat the Passover meal with His beloved disciples. Therefore, He planned to eat it with them early, on the thirteenth day of the month of Nisan.

H. D. M. Spence explains a threefold purpose for the intense longing of Jesus to celebrate this last Passover with His disciples. He longs to bid them farewell, as we would with our loved ones if we knew we were dying tomorrow. He longs to instruct them. And He longs, as the Founder of the one true religion, to transform the Passover feast of deliverance into a supper which will commemorate a far greater deliverance.[40]

8. Read Exodus 12:1–30 and answer the following:

A. What were the Israelites instructed to do in verses 5–7?

B. What parallel do you see with Christ?

C. Why were they to continue to observe this supper every year? (vv. 24–28)

Read Luke 22:7–20.

9. At what point does Jesus transform the Passover meal into a supper which will commemorate a far greater deliverance?

When we take Communion, we can look backward to Passover, and forward to an even greater meal (v. 18). What is it? (See Revelation 19:9.)

Personal Action Assignment

Not only were the Israelites delivered from death, but from slavery. Is there an "enslaving" habit (anger, gluttony...) from which Christ's power has set you free? Fall to your knees and ask Jesus to deliver you from that spirit of addiction and to replace it with a spirit of joy and peace.

Check out a free internet Bible study for those enslaved with any kind of addiction (gluttony, alcohol, pornography, gambling...) I recommend it highly: http://www.settingcaptivesfree.com

DAY 4

Satan Entered Judas

In *The Screwtape Letters*, C. S. Lewis says, "There are two equal and opposite errors into which our race can fall about the devils. One is to disbelieve in their existence. The other is to believe, and to feel an excessive and unhealthy interest in them."[41]

Certainly Luke 22 makes it clear Satan is real, and that we had better be alert!

Read Luke 22:1–7.

10. Why was Jerusalem so crowded, and why did this present a difficulty for the chief priests and officers of the temple guard? (Compare Luke 19:47–48.)

How did Judas help them with their dilemma? Why do you think they rejoiced?

11. What lies might Satan have possibly whispered to Judas to tempt the betrayal?

12. Judas certainly stands as a warning that proximity to Jesus and His followers is not enough—Jesus wants our hearts! What warning does Jesus give in Luke 6:43–49?

13. It is easy to deceive ourselves and think we are obeying when we are really just hearing. How do we know? By fruit. Examine the following branches of your life and see if there is consistently good fruit:

    A. Relationships (husband, in-laws, friends, family, other)

    B. Habits (quiet time, eating, housekeeping, choice of entertainment, other)

    C. Compassion (the unsaved, the hungry, the hurting)

Read Luke 22:21–23.

14. Though Jesus' death is destined, Judas is still personally responsible for the betrayal. How does Jesus express this here?

15. What else does Jesus tell us in Matthew 26:24? What does this mean?

16. How does Judas show his hypocrisy in Matthew 26:25?

17. How does Judas show his hypocrisy in Luke 22:47–48?

18. Hypocrisy is a sin that tempts us when we long for the praise of men instead of the praise of God, when we are building our own little kingdom instead of the kingdom of God. Show how this is true in the following:

    A. Luke 11:37–42

    B. Luke 20:46–47

19. Do you long for the praise of men or of God?

Which is wiser? Why?

Review your memory verse.

Personal Action Assignment

Pray for protection for yourself and your loved ones. Pray that you will desire the praise of God, and not of men, for one of Satan's frequent lures is the praise of men. (See Luke 4:5–7.)

DAY 5
....

Simon, Simon, Satan Has Asked to Sift You

When we are strong, we are dangerous in Satan's eyes. Peter was bold—he was the leader. Ken Gire, in *Intimate Moments with the Savior,* describes it like this:

> Satan wants to thresh his faith and beat it into the ground until the husk breaks open. Then he'll show the world what's really inside Peter's heart. And once the other disciples see this, the backbone of the revolution will be as good as crushed.[42]

20. Summarize the following passages:

    A. Matthew 27:1–5

    B. Luke 22:31–32

    C. Luke 22:33–34

    D. Luke 22:54–62

    E. John 21:15–19

21. Judas was lost, but Peter reinstated. Both were sad about their sin, so what do you think made the difference? (See 2 Corinthians 7:9–10.)

How do you respond when you have given and given to someone and then they hurt you?

Most of us withdraw. We think: "How could she do this? If she really loved me, if she really appreciated all I have done for her, then she wouldn't have hurt me." And yet, if we are honest, we know that we have hurt people we love deeply.

Jesus kept on loving. Jesus gave grace.

22. Describe how Jesus responds to those who hurt Him:

    A. Luke 22:42

    B. Luke 22:45–46

    C. Luke 22:47–48

    D. Luke 22:49–51

    E. Luke 24:34

23. Describe one time when you have let Jesus down. How did He respond?

What does God ask of us in Ephesians 4:32?

24. How has God spoken to you through this lesson?

Prayer Time

Instead of sharing individual prayer requests, have each woman lift her own request up in prayer. Then have a few women support her with sentences. When there is a silence, another woman should lift up her individual prayer request.

Eleventh Stop!
Do Not Weep for Me

Throughout his Gospel Luke emphasizes: *Jesus is the Christ sent for all people!*

Remember what the angel said at the beginning of Luke's Gospel? Good news for all people! Yet not all will receive this good news. Here, at the end of Jesus' earthly life, you will see a wide spectrum of responses to Him.

You cannot remain neutral, though you may try, as Pilate did, but ultimately you will be held accountable for your failure to totally embrace Him. Whether you are a man or a woman, Jew or Gentile, rich or poor—indifference is as dangerous as opposition. Judgment awaits those who are hard or soft in their rejection of the Christ. Max Lucado says: "As long as you can take him or leave him, you might as well leave him, because he won't be taken halfheartedly."[43]

This man, despised and broken, is the Messiah. Dr. Darrell Bock says: "If there is one thing that Luke is after in his Gospel, it is the need to totally embrace the Innocent One who died."[44] If you have not embraced Jesus, take the following words of Jesus to heart:

> *Daughters of Jerusalem, do not weep for me; weep for yourselves and for your children* (Luke 23:28).

Prepare Your Heart to Hear
Each day, before you begin, ask God to speak personally to you. Write what impresses you in your journal.

Memory Work

Review Luke 23:28. During the next two weeks complete:

> *He said to them, "Why are you troubled, and why do doubts rise in your minds? Look at my hands and my feet. It is I myself! Touch me and see; a ghost does not have flesh and bones, as you see I have."*
>
> Luke 24:38–39

WARMUP

Call out some words which describe responses you have seen to Jesus. What do you think is the most common?

DAY I

Overview—Part I

Read Luke 21—22.

The death and resurrection of Jesus shows us He was much more than a great moral teacher. Yet that is how many in the world define Him. Perhaps they do so out of ignorance, or perhaps, like Pilate, they are trying to be positive toward Jesus without wholeheartedly embracing Him. However, this response is not logical. In *Mere Christianity*, C. S. Lewis explains:

> *A man who was merely a man and said the sort of things Jesus said would not be a great moral teacher. He would either be a lunatic—on a level with the man who says he is a poached egg—or else he would be the Devil of Hell.* [45]

Lewis puts this in allegory form in *The Lion, the Witch, and the Wardrobe*. Lucy has come out of the wardrobe with a fantastic story about discovering another world—and her siblings dismiss her story as preposterous. The professor responds:

> *"Logic!" said the Professor half to himself. "Why don't they teach logic at these schools? There are only three possibilities. Either your sister is telling lies, or she is mad, or she is telling the truth. You know she doesn't tell lies and it is obvious that she is not mad. For the moment then and unless any further evidence turns up, we must assume that she is telling the truth."* [46]

1. What stood out to you from the introduction for The Eleventh Stop! Do Not Weep for Me (p. 109)

2. What stood out to you from the introduction for Day 1 (p. 118)?

Read Luke 22:63 through Luke 23:31.

3. Describe who responded to Jesus and how. Note also any response of Jesus in return.

   A. Luke 22:63–65

   B. Luke 22:66–71

   C. Luke 23:1–7

   D. Luke 23:8–11

   E. Luke 23:13–25

   F. Luke 23:27

4. Summarize the above negative responses to Jesus. What impresses you about the way Jesus responds? Sing "When I Survey the Wondrous Cross" from your hymnal. Learn your memory passage.

DAY 2

Overview—Part II

He could have called ten thousand, but He chose to die for you and me.

5. Describe who responded to Jesus and how.

   A. Luke 23:35–37

   B. Luke 23:39

   C. Luke 23:40–43

   D. Luke 23:47

   E. Luke 23:50–53

   F. Luke 23:55–56

6. Which of the above responded positively to Jesus? How does Luke show by this that the good news is for all people?

Spend five minutes on your memory passage.
Sing "Hallelujah, What a Savior!" from your hymnal.

DAY 3

Herod and Pilate Became Friends

What made friends of two former enemies? Their rejection of Christ! Their rejection was different: Herod mocked Christ and Pilate tried to wash his hands of Him (Matthew 27:24), but the result was the same. They rejected the Innocent One God had sent and they will be judged.

It's intriguing to trace the response of Pilate to Jesus. He had many warnings. Even his wife warned him:

> *While Pilate was sitting on the judge's seat, his wife sent him this message: "Don't have anything to do with that innocent man, for I have suffered a great deal today in a dream because of him."*
>
> Matthew 27:19

Pilate did what he did out of fear. It's helpful to know that Pilate's predecessor was put to death for falling out of grace with his political superior, Caesar. See how the crowd preys upon Pilate's fear of Caesar.

7. A. What does the crowd tell Pilate in Luke 23:1–2?

   B. Was it true that Jesus opposed paying taxes? (See Luke 20:20–26)

   C. How does Jesus respond to the charge of being King of the Jews?

8. What other details does John give us concerning the reply of Jesus to Pilate in John 18:36–37?

What enigmatic reply does Pilate make to this in John 18:38a?

Moral relativists are not new!

9. How does Pilate try to escape judging Jesus? (Luke 23:6–7) Is he successful? (Luke 23:11)

10. When Jesus comes back to Pilate, how does Pilate try to appease the crowd? (Luke 23:16)

Pilate keeps trying to wriggle out of his corner. The other Gospel writers give us more detail here.

11. Describe what happens in Matthew 27:21–26.

12. In John 19:7–16 describe:
    A. Pilate's fear (John 19:8)

    B. Jesus' response (John 19:11)

    Contrary to what many evangelicals believe, there are degrees of sin. Pilate was sinning, and he would be held guilty, but in John 19:11 Jesus tells Pilate that the one who handed him over to Pilate was guilty of the greater sin. However, all sin deserves death, and the fact that we may have sinned less than some will not help us on Judgment Day. Matthew Henry says that it will not "avail in the great day to say others were worse than we."[47]

13. Fearing man or God:
    A. What method finally gives the crowd success with Pilate in John 19:12?

    B. How does the thief on the cross show greater wisdom than Pilate? (Luke 23:40a)

    C. What does Jesus tell us in Luke 12:5?

    D. Give some situations in which your fear of man might keep you from doing what is best.

DAY 4

Daughters of Jerusalem

The term "Daughters of Jerusalem" or "Daughters of Zion" (Zion is interchangeable with Jerusalem as Zion is the mountain on which Jerusalem is built) refers to the daughters which live in that city. When the phrase is singular ("Daughter of Jerusalem") it means the city, for cities, though they include males and females, are usually considered feminine. However, when it is written in the plural ("Daughters of Jerusalem"), it seems to be directed toward just the women. This happens in three different books: Isaiah, Song of Songs, and Luke.

In Song of Songs, the Daughters of Jerusalem are continually asking questions of the bride, as they are enthralled and curious about her love for her lover and his love for her. Many commentators, such as Charles Spurgeon and Matthew Henry, believe that the Song of Songs, in addition to being a portrait of the beauty of married love, is also a reflection of the beauty of the love between Christ and His bride, the true church. It seems to me that in the Song of Songs the Daughters of Jerusalem are curious and enchanted, but do not necessarily embrace Christ themselves. It is possible to be enchanted by religion: by Christmas carols, midnight mass, stained-glass windows, and angels and yet, miss Jesus.

In Isaiah, the Daughters of Zion were far from God, even though they lived right in Jerusalem. Simply being close to the truth, being the daughter of a pastor, raised in the church, or living in a spiritual mecca like Wheaton, Colorado Springs, or Jerusalem does not mean that you know Jesus. God is holy and He will punish sin. We all need to repent, embrace the Savior, and bear fruit worthy of repentance.

In the New Testament, the term "Daughters of Jerusalem" occurs only in Luke. Here again, though, the women are not hostile to Jesus; they have missed the truth. Seeing His torn flesh and bleeding brow, they sympathize with His suffering. But Jesus turns to them and says: "Weep not for me, weep for yourselves." There are many today who consider themselves believers, yet they have not mourned for their own sin and turned around to wholeheartedly embrace Jesus as Lord. Dr. Darrell Bock says: "Not all opposition to Jesus is hard opposition."[48]

14. Summarize what you learned from the above about the "Daughters of Jerusalem."

What stood out to you personally? Why?

15. Describe the "Daughters" in the following passages. These women were missing something important. Explain what you see.

   A. Isaiah 3:16–24

   B. Luke 23:27–28

God's love and protection for women should not lull us into complacency, into the false belief that only men will be held accountable for living wholeheartedly for Christ. Jesus certainly makes this clear in His exhortation to the Daughters of

Jerusalem. It isn't enough for women to hear God's Word (Luke 8:21), nor is it enough to feel emotion about God, as the Daughters of Jerusalem did. We must wake up and walk in the light all day long.

16. Is His spirit speaking to you in any way from the above? If so, how?

Review your memory work of Luke 24:28-39.

Sing "Living for Jesus" from your hymnal.

DAY 5

Judgment and Our Response

In the passages you will study today you will read of judgment. When the prophets, including Jesus, talked about judgment it usually referred to both a near and a distant judgment. Jesus warns of the fall of Jerusalem, which did occur in AD 70 It was just as Jesus prophesied here and in Luke 20. Jerusalem was surrounded. Women and little children were victims as well. The terror was great. There is a pattern, for one day the terror of the final judgment will be great.

17. Have you ever personally experienced a natural disaster such as an earthquake, a flood, or a tornado? If so, share some of your feelings, or what you imagine your feelings would be.

18. Why does Jesus weep over Jerusalem in the following passages? What phrases reveal His compassion?

A. Luke 13:34–35

B. Luke 19:41–44

C. Luke 21:20–24

Prophecy is meant to warn us. When the Roman armies were gathering in AD 70, the Christian congregations remembered the words of Jesus spoken here and fled to Pella beyond Jordan.[49] May we, likewise, believe God's warning of the coming judgment and become, not just good women, but excellent and pure women of God. Jesus continues now with a distant prophecy, showing God's pattern in judgment.

19. In Luke 21:25–36
    A. What will be the cosmic signs that the end is near? (v. 25)

    B. How will people respond? (v. 26)

    C. How will Jesus arrive? (v. 27)

    D. How should we respond to this warning? (vv. 34–36)

20. Why were the people in charge of the *Titanic,* and also of the *Challenger,* complacent? What warnings did they ignore? What proper precautions did they fail to take?

21. Why are people, even believers, complacent about the coming judgment? What warnings (21:34–35) are they ignoring? What proper precautions are they failing to take? (21:36)

Luke has shown us a variety of negative responses to Jesus, some hard, some soft, but all resulting in judgment. There is the hard rejection of the religious leaders, the frivolity of Herod, spinelessness of Pilate, and the misdirected weeping of the Daughters of Jerusalem.

Now Luke closes his passion account with responses of faith.

22. Although the thief on the cross did not utter a traditional "sinner's prayer," his response brought him forgiveness. What do you see in his response? What do you learn from Jesus' words? (Luke 23:40–43)

23. How did the centurion respond? (Luke 23:47) Review Luke 23 and record what the centurion might have witnessed that led him to his response of faith.

24. Luke describes certain individuals as good and righteous, among them Zechariah, Elizabeth, Simeon, Anna, and now Joseph of Arimathea. What did Joseph of Arimathea do? What does this tell you about him? (Luke 23:50–54)

John 19:39 tells us that Nicodemus helped Joseph and that they anointed Him with 75 pounds of spices, the amount usually reserved for a king. [50]

25. What do you see that is commendable in the women who had come with Jesus? (Luke 23:55–56)

Contrast their responses to the disciples and to the Daughters of Jerusalem.

26. What do you think you will remember from this lesson?

How could you apply it to your life?

Prayer Time

Pray first for urgent needs. Then spend time in prayer for each other to become pure and excellent women of God. In groups of four or five, choose a leader who will lift up the name of each woman in your circle to God. Then whoever feels prompted should lift up a short sentence prayer for that woman. When there is a silence, the leader should lift up the name of the next woman. Some Scriptures that might guide you in praying for each other are Philippians 1:9–11 and Titus 2:3–5.

Last Stop!
A Slow Dawning

It has the ring of truth. Instead of confidently believing, they grope about in half-light, slowly coming to the truth, like the dim-witted creatures we all truly are.

The women:
They wonder …
They are frightened, yet filled with joy …
Then they remember His words …
The disciples:
The women's words seem like nonsense.
Peter saw the strips of linen lying by themselves …
he went away, wondering …

I love the escalating drama. Luke alone paints the beautiful portrait of the two on the road to Emmaus. Here again, they are puzzled, confused, even angry! There is humor as Jesus joins them and they do not recognize Him. Instead, they vent their emotions. And He shares from the Word with them, widening their light, causing their hearts to burn within them. And then, when He dines with them, their eyes are opened! They see!

Oh, can it be? Yes! He is risen! HE IS RISEN INDEED!

Prepare Your Heart to Hear
Each day, ask God to help you recognize Him, as He did for the two on the road to Emmaus!

Memory Work
Complete Luke 24:38–39:

> He said to them, "Why are you troubled, and why do doubts rise in your minds? Look at my hands and my feet. It is I myself! Touch me and see; a ghost does not have flesh and bones, as you see I have."

Warmup
Think about the dearest person to you on earth. Imagine he (or she) died cruelly and unexpectedly. And then, on the third day, you heard he was alive. How do you think you would react? Why?

DAY 1
. . . .

Overview
Read Luke 23—24.

In *The Jesus I Never Knew,* Philip Yancey says "The crowd challenged Jesus to prove himself by climbing down from the cross, but not one person thought of what actually would happen: that he would die and come back." The surprise that morning is great. "Accounts of the empty tomb sound breathless and fragmentary...Surely conspirators could have done a neater job of depicting what they would later claim to be a huge hinge of history...unless of course they were not concocting a legend but recording the plain facts."[51]

Read Luke 24.

1. As you read, observe the confusion, the bewilderment, the slowly dawning light. Find examples like the one given:

Who	*What*	*Why*
women	wondering	the stone rolled away and the body gone

Review your memory work.

DAY 2
. . . .

Resurrection Discovered
Of all the major religions, only Christianity values women. All through His life Jesus defied the culture and reached out to women, shocking the men around Him. Historian Flavius Josephus reflects the prejudice of the day when he writes:

"Let not the testimony of women be admitted, on account of the levity and bold-ness of their sex."[52] All four Gospel writers record women as being the first at the empty tomb! Philip Yancey says no conspirator in the first century would have invented *that!* But the truth is, God allowed women to be there first, to be the first to see Jesus, to be the first to tell the amazing story.[53]

Read Luke 24:1–12.

2. Why do you think God allowed women to be at the tomb first? As a woman, what does this mean to you?

3. While the women were wondering about the missing body, what happened? Describe what they saw and heard.

4. How was the third day the day of salvation in these passages?

   A. Genesis 22:4

   B. Genesis 42:17–18

   C. Esther 5:1

   D. Hosea 6:2

   E. Jonah 1:17

   F. Luke 24:7, 21, 45

5. What significance do you see in the above pattern?

6. The women reported *everything.* What would that include? How did the apos-tles respond?

The "nonsense" is a word used in medical settings of the delirious talk of the very ill![54]

DAY 3

We Had Hoped Jesus Was the One!

This beautiful story, told in detail by Luke alone, is filled with suspense, drama, and humor. Cleopas and another believer are on the road to Emmaus, sharing their confusion and disappointment, when Jesus joins them. They do not recognize Him, but pour out their disappointment to Him. Walter Wangerin imagines it like this:

> *As soon as Cleopas glanced at him, the stranger said, "Friends, what are you talking about?"*
>
> *All at once Cleopas' daughter stopped and put her head down and began to cry. Until that moment it had not occurred to him that she would be as sorrowful as he ... Cleopas, hearing such despair in his young daughter, suddenly realized who he was angry at.*
>
> *"This morning an idiot woman told us that the grave was empty and that Jesus was alive," he said. "Simon went and looked. They were right. The grave was empty. But that means absolutely nothing. And he who caused us to hope has now become the death of hope! Jesus, Teacher, Messiah ... pah! That is what that dead man taught me: to hate life because everything is vanity and nothing is more than a striving after wind!"*
>
> *Cleopas was furious with Jesus.*
>
> *"Ah, you foolish fellow," the stranger said, "slow to believe what the prophets have spoken!"*
>
> *If his daughter hadn't put her arms around him and held him so tightly, Cleopas would have hit the man.*
>
> *Softly, earnestly, she asked, "What did the prophets say?"* 55

Read Luke 24:13–35.

7. In this story, what emotions do you see? (Give references.) Look carefully at the scripture text and also try to identify with the characters. *Why* do you think they would be feeling what they seemed to be feeling in each case?

8. What did Jesus do in both Luke 24:27 and 24:44–45?

What caused you to place your trust in Christ? One of the evidences that persuaded my sister Sally was the change in the apostles from a ragged band who were hiding out to a fearless army, willing to be martyred for the truth. For me, it was, in part, the prophecies. I can identify with the two on the road to Emmaus, whose hearts burned within them as Jesus opened the Scriptures to them! But it is also clear that we recognized Jesus because He opened our eyes.

9. What common theme do you see in the following?
   A. Luke 9:45

   B. Luke 18:34

   C. Luke 24:16

   D. Luke 24:31

How exciting it must have been to be these two disciples. Which Scriptures from Moses, the Psalms, and the Prophets did Jesus show them? Wouldn't you love to know? I would!

Dr. Darrell Bock told me we may have a clue because the early sermons by the apostles, as recorded by Luke in Acts, are laced with Scriptures from Moses, the Psalms, and the Prophets! As you look at them, ask God to open your eyes, the way He did for the two on the road to Emmaus! (Turn in your hymnal and sing: "Open My Eyes That I May See.")

10. Look carefully at each of these verses in Acts (*and the context*) and then look at its original source. On the basis of what the apostles are saying, how do you think Jesus might have explained these Old Testament Scriptures to their fellow believers on the road to Emmaus?

    A. Acts 3:22 (Deut. 18:15)

Dr. Bock thinks Jesus may have begun with this verse. Why would this be a logical starting place?

    B. Acts 4:11 (Ps. 118:22)

    C. Acts 4:25–26 (Ps. 2:1–2)

    D. Acts 2:34–35 (Ps. 110:1)

This psalm is quoted extensively in the New Testament. It affirms the Deity of Jesus and His eternal priesthood.

    E. Acts 2:17 (Joel 2:28–32)

    F. Acts 13:33 (Ps. 2:7)

    G. Acts 13:35 (Ps. 16:10)

    H. Acts 13:47 (Isa. 49:6)

11. What truths impressed you from the above questions?

DAY 4

A Ghost Has Not Flesh and Bones

In Billy Graham's autobiography, *Just As I Am*, he tells of a man coming to his wife's door and claiming to be Jesus. "'Well,'" Ruth responded, "why did you have to knock? Why didn't you just come in through the closed door?" He stopped and scratched his head, then got back in his car and drove down the mountain.[56]

Can you imagine how the disciples felt when Jesus suddenly stood among them? (John tells us the door was locked!) The disciples thought they were seeing a ghost! And Jesus read their minds and reassured them by letting them touch Him, by watching Him eat!

Read Luke 24:36–49.

12. Describe the feelings you think the disciples had and why.

13. In the following passages, how do you see John and Peter reflecting back to these days?
    A. 2 Peter 1:16

    B. 1 John 1:1–3

14. What commission does Jesus give them in Luke 24:46–49?

The disciples are not abandoned but commissioned. In a world where many do not know their place, identity, or purpose, the resurrection means that disciples can know that God is at work, that Jesus is alive in glory, and that death is not the end.

Darrell Bock [57]

15. Describe the Ascension in Luke 24:50–53. Imagine being there. What would be your feelings?

16. How is your life different because of the events described in Luke 24?

In your personal quiet time sing "Because He Lives" from your hymnal and spend some time giving thanks to Him.

DAY 5

The Take-Away

At the first writing seminar I attended, I was asked: "What will be the 'take-away' from your book?" The take-away is what the reader will remember from a book long after she has closed the cover.

Certain themes prevailed in Luke's Gospel, themes which he wanted you to take away! In answering these questions, be a ponderer, like Mary the mother of Jesus, like Mary of Bethany. You may very well double the impact of this study on your life by the value you place on this final day.

17. Luke wanted you to know WHO Jesus is. Find several key scenes from Luke that proclaim or show the identity of Jesus.

18. Luke wanted you to know that Jesus came for ALL people. Give examples of each from Luke. Find several key scenes to show Jesus came for Jews, for Gentiles, for women, and for children.

19. Luke wanted you to know how you fit into God's plan. The plan for believers begins in Luke and continues in Acts. (At one point, Luke and Acts were one book.) Being attentive to God's Spirit and responding in faith are crucial. Recall a few women who exemplified this. What did they do that made them stand out? Be specific, for this is key for your life.

20. Review your notes and summarize your take-away for:

THE FIRST OASIS: The Savior's Birth

THE SECOND OASIS: The Savior's Power

THE THIRD OASIS: The Savior's Wisdom

THE FOURTH OASIS: The Savior's Victory

Prayer Time

Write down two ways you would like to grow in godliness. Share those and then pray for one another in this regard!

Sources

THE FIRST OASIS: The Savior's Birth

1. Darrell L. Bock, *Luke,* Vol. 1. 1:1–9:50 (Grand Rapids: Baker, 1994), 111.
2. Luci Shaw, "Yes to Shame and Glory," *Christianity Today*. Dec. 1986, 22.
3. Walter Wangerin, Jr., *The Book of God: The Bible as a Novel* (Grand Rapids: Zondervan, 1996), 580–81.
4. R.M. Edgar, "Luke." *The Pulpit Commentary*, Vol. 16. Ed. H. D. M. Spence and Joseph S. Excell (Peabody, MA.: Hendrickson, n.d.), 35.
5. Dee Brestin, *The Friendships of Women* (Colorado Springs: Chariot Victor, 1997), 164.
6. W. Clarkson, "Luke." *The Pulpit Commentary*, 54.
7. Bock, *Luke,* p. 250.
8. Philip Yancey, *The Jesus I Never Knew* (Grand Rapids: Zondervan, 1995), 43.
9. Amy Carmichael, *Candles in the Dark* (Fort Washington, PA: Christian Literature Crusade, 1982), 52.
10. Evelyn Bence, *Mary's Journal: A Mother's Story* (New York: Harper, 1992), 139–41.

THE SECOND OASIS: The Savior's Power

11. Philip Yancey, *The Jesus I Never Knew*, 21.
12. Francis A. Schaeffer, *The Church at the End of the Twentieth Century* (Downers Grove, IL: InterVarsity, 1970), 138–39.
13. Darrell L. Bock, *Luke*, Vol. 1, 652.
14. Ibid., 713–14.
15. Ken Gire, *Intimate Moments with the Savior: Learning to Love* (Grand Rapids: Zondervan, 1989), 48–49.
16. Darrell L. Bock, *Luke*, Vol. 1, 786.

THE THIRD OASIS: The Savior's Wisdom

17. Dorothy Sayers, as quoted by Philip Yancey, *The Jesus I Never Knew*, 154.
18. Walter Wangerin, Jr., *The Book of God*, 550-551.
19. Dr. S. Conway, "The Psalms." *The Pulpit Commentary*, Vol. 8, 255.
20. Dennis Cauchon, "Childhood Pastimes Are Increasingly Moving Indoors," *USA Today*, July 12, 2005, front page.
21. Josh Harris, "Thanks Mom and Dad," *New Attitude*, Vol. 4, no. 4, n.d., 39.
22. Frederica Mathewes-Green, "Compassion," *Virtue*, March/April 1997.
23. Darrell L. Bock, *Jesus According to Scripture*, (Grand Rapids: Baker, 2002) 258.
24. Ibid.
25. Billy Graham, *Just As I Am: The Autobiography of Billy Graham* (New York: Harper Collins, 1997), n. p.
26. Alan Redpath, *Victorious Christian Service* (Westwood, NJ: Revell, 1958), 23.

27. Darrell L. Bock, *Luke*, Vol. 2, 9:51–24:53 (Grand Rapids: Baker, 1996), 1063.
28. Darrell L. Bock, *Jesus According to Scripture*, 266.
29. Ibid. p. 284.
30. Barbara Brown Taylor, *The Preaching Life* (Cambridge, MA: Cowley, 1993), 147–48.
31. John Stott, *Christian Mission in the Modern World* (Downers Grove, IL: InterVarsity, 1975), 81.
32. Philip Yancey, *What's So Amazing about Grace?* (Grand Rapids: Zondervan, 1997), 11.
33. Jim Wallis, as quoted in Philip Yancey, *What's So Amazing about Grace?*, 2.
34. Helmut Thielicke, *The Waiting Father*, trans. by John W. Doberstein (New York: Harper, 1959), 24–26.

THE FOURTH OASIS: The Savior's Victory

35. C.S. Lewis, *The Lion, the Witch, and the Wardrobe* (New York: Harper Trophy, 1978), 168, 170, 178.
36. Walter Wink, as quoted in Philip Yancey, *The Jesus I Never Knew*, 284.
37. Elisabeth Elliot, *A Chance to Die: The Life and Legacy of Amy Carmichael* (Grand Rapids: Revell, 1987), 64.
38. Darrell L. Bock, *Luke*, Vol. 2, 1706.
39. Luci Shaw, *God in the Dark: Through Grief and Beyond* (Grand Rapids: Broadmoor, 1989), 63.
40. H. D. M. Spence, "Luke." *The Pulpit Commentary*, 197–98.
41. C. S. Lewis, *The Screwtape Letters & Screwtape Proposes a Toast* (New York: Macmillan, 1961), 3.
42. Ken Gire, *Intimate Moments with the Savior: Learning to Love*, 98.
43. Max Lucado, *The Applause of Heaven* (Dallas: Word, 1996).
44. Darrell L. Bock, *Luke,* Vol. 2, 1867.
45. C. S. Lewis, *Mere Christianity* (New York: Macmillan, 1964), 40–41.
46. C. S. Lewis, *The Lion, the Witch, and the Wardrobe*, 51–52.
47. Matthew Henry, "Matthew to John." *Matthew Henry's Commentary on the Whole Bible*, Vol. 5. (Peabody, MA: Hendrickson, 1991), 963.
48. Darrell L. Bock, *Luke*, Vol. 2, 1845.
49. H. D. M. Spence, "Luke." *The Pulpit Commentary*, 185.
50. Darrell L. Bock, Luke. Vol. 2, 1875.
51. Philip Yancey, *The Jesus I Never Knew*, 212–13.
52. Flavius Josephus, "The Antiquities of the Jews." *Josephus: Complete Works*, trans. by William Whiston (Grand Rapids: Kregel, 1981), 97.
53. Philip Yancey, *The Jesus I Never Knew*, 212.
54. A. Plummer, as quoted in Darrell L. Bock, *Luke*, Vol. 2, 1898.
55. Walter Wangerin, Jr., *The Book of God*, 822–23.
56. Billy Graham, *Just As I Am*, 668.
57. Darrell L. Bock, *Luke*, Vol. 2, 1923.